HAYNES MAX POWER

ICe

The definitive guide to **in-car entertainment**

by **Andy Butler**

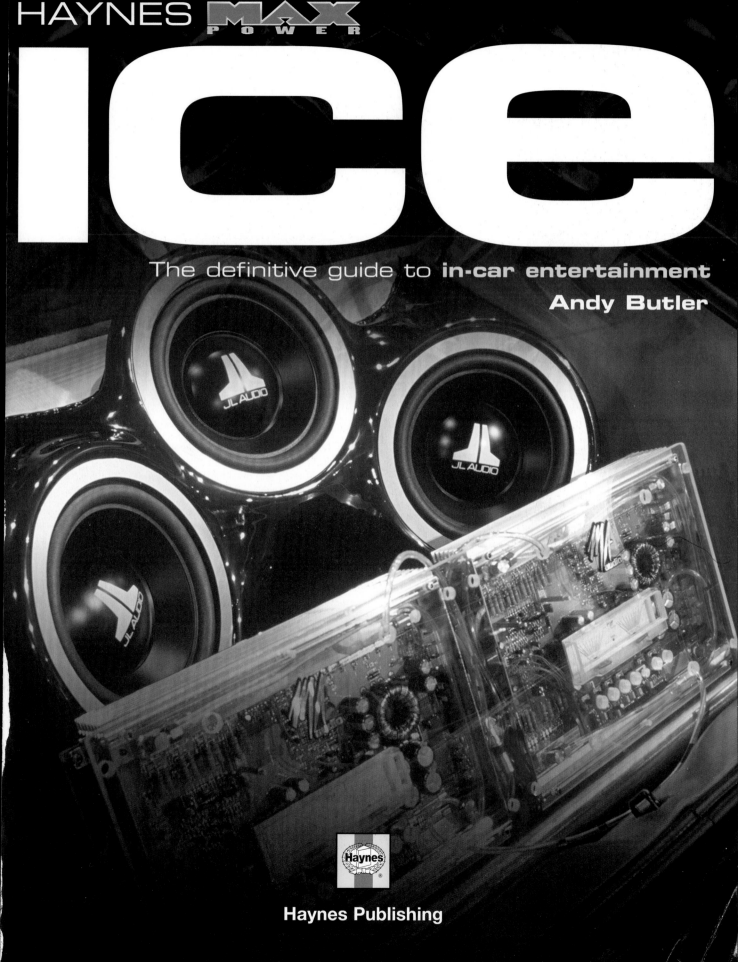

HAYNES MAX POWER

ice

The definitive guide to **in-car entertainment**

Andy Butler

Haynes

Haynes Publishing

© Andy Butler 2002

ISBN 1 85960 836 1

Printed by **J H Haynes & Co Ltd,**
Sparkford, Yeovil, Somerset BA22 7JJ, England.

Tel: 01963 442030 Fax: 01963 440001
Int. tel: +44 1963 442030 Fax: +44 1963 440001
E-mail: sales@haynes-manuals.co.uk
Web site: www.haynes.co.uk

Haynes North America, Inc
861 Lawrence Drive, Newbury Park, California 91320, USA

Editions Haynes S.A.
Tour Aurore IBC - La Défense 2, 18 Place des Reflets,
92975 PARIS LA DEFENSE Cedex, France

Haynes Publishing Nordiska AB
Box 1504, 751 45 UPPSALA, Sweden

Disclaimer

1 Advice on safety procedures and precautions is contained in this manual. You are strongly recommended to note these comments, and to pay close attention to any instructions that may be given by the parts supplier.

2 If, after reading this manual, you are still unsure as to how to go about the modification, advice should be sought from a competent and experienced individual. Any queries regarding modification should be addressed to the product manufacturer concerned, and not to J H Haynes, nor the vehicle manufacturer.

3 The instructions in this manual are followed at the risk of the reader who remains fully and solely responsible for the safety, roadworthiness and legality of his/her vehicle. Thus J H Haynes are giving only non-specific advice in this respect.

4 When modifying a car it is important to bear in mind the legal responsibilities placed on the owners, driver and modifiers of cars, including, but not limited to, the Road Traffic Act 1988. IN PARTICULAR, IT IS AN OFFENCE TO DRIVE ON A PUBLIC ROAD A VEHICLE WHICH IS NOT INSURED OR WHICH DOES NOT COMPLY WITH THE CONSTRUCTION AND USE REGULATIONS, OR WHICH IS DANGEROUS AND MAY CAUSE INJURY TO ANY PERSON.

5 Any advice provided is correct to the best of our knowledge at the time of publication, but the reader should pay particular attention to any changes of specification to the vehicles, or parts, which can occur without notice.

6 Alterations to vehicles should be disclosed to insurers, and legal advice taken from the police, or appropriate regulatory bodies.

7 Readers should not assume that the vehicle manufacturers have given their approval to the modifications carried out within this manual.

8 Neither J H Haynes nor the manufacturers give any warranty as to the safety of a vehicle after alterations, such as those contained in this book, have been made. J H Haynes will not accept liability for any economic loss, damage to property or death and personal injury arising from use of this manual other than in respect of injury or death resulting directly from J H Haynes' negligence.

Acknowledgements

This is the section where I get to say Ta Very Much to all those poor people I pestered for answers, that I borrowed kit from, and who put up with me rabbiting on about getting this book finished when I should have been doing something else.

Firstly, I have to thank my wife, Zoë Harrison for taking almost every photograph in the book. Then there was the proof-reading, spell checking, continuity checking. The list of jobs just goes on and on. Her name really should be at the front with mine

Next I have to thank all the people from the car audio companies who helped get information, equipment and other details to me in time for the book to be finished on its ultra-tight deadline. Without this back-up, you'd be holding a lot of empty pages. So, thanks - in company alphabetical order, so no squabbling - go to:

Keith and Cheryl at Alpine Electronics UK Ltd, who bring you Alpine equipment

James at Audioscape, for those funky custom-fit bass boxes and door builds

Paul at Auto Acoustics, makers of the MDF replacement shelves, custom-fit enclosures and perspex panelling

Glen and Tracy at Autoleads Ltd, for all the fitting bits, wiring accessories and Kicker

Gordon, Geoff and Matt at BBG Distribution Ltd, purveyors of Dynamat, JL Audio, Nakamichi in-car, Phoenix Gold and MTX

John, Gary, Mark and Dean at Clifford DEI Ltd - so that'll be Directed and Clifford, then

Steve at Focal JM Lab UK, no need to guess there, that's Focal

Ro at Gamepath - they do the business with JBL and Infinity gear

Gordon at Genesis I.C.E. Ltd - that's an easy one, Genesis, and also Select Products stuff

Simon at Hayden Labs Ltd - MB Quart and Audiovox, in case you were wondering

Tony at InCars magazine for archived stuff

Lucio, Maria, Manville, Steve, Don, Gary, Kris, Hector, Bill and everyone else at JL Audio in sunny Florida

Dan at Redline magazine for more piccies

Chris at Total Car Audio for finding more archived shots

Alan at The Vintage Wireless Company for providing the antiques to photograph

To Special Interest Publishing Director Mark Hughes for letting me loose on the project in the first place; to Project Manager Louise McIntyre for munching as many stress sandwiches as I have while putting the whole thing together, and to Copy Editor Peter McSean for editing the copy...

And finally to my mates Steve Dowd and Simon Stephenson for letting us rip their cars apart to do some of the install work. Hope you enjoyed the bacon sarnies while we were doing the jobs, and are enjoying the choons now. Cheers.

This book has been brought to you in part by the phrases 'Damn, I nearly cut me finger off!' and 'What d'you mean hold still while you reload the camera?' and the products Solstis, Thornton's Special Toffee, Dial-A-Curry and Andy's Patent Eyelid Props. Ay thang yew...

Dedication

This book is dedicated to my wife Zoë for all the work she did on it. I couldn't have finished this project at all without her spending as much time as I did in the workshop, hanging around until I said 'here's a bit to shoot', when she could have been doing something much more interesting instead...

Contents

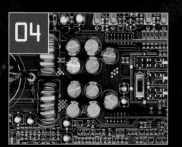

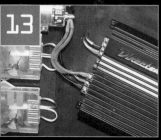

In-car entertainment has come a long way since the days of the wireless. And, just like the cars they're fitted to, the biggest jumps in quality and sophistication seem to have been crammed into the last few years.

Not only have units become far more clever, they've also become incredibly cheap. A really good system is now within the reach of just

In the beginning

about anyone who can afford a car in the first place – and we don't mean just because everyone's got several credit cards. Things truly have never been cheaper. But it hasn't always been like this.

Cars have been around for more than 100 years now, yet motorists had to wait until the early 1930s for some form of wireless musical accompaniment. Until then, in-car entertainment meant something completely different and it wasn't talked about in polite company.

In fact, the first car radios were of more use when the car was parked rather than moving. They did get better, though, and soon became more sophisticated. Even so, we're only talking about pushbutton radio tuning. It was some time later before the driver could enjoy his or her own music selection on the move.

When the first autotuning radio arrived, it used a wickedly clever clockwork mechanism rather than the digital type that's common today. The old unit's preset buttons needed a healthy shove to move the tuner settings, but pushing the autoseek control had the pointer whirring up the scale until it hit the next programmed station.

For an alternative to the radio stations' output, the only choice was to play a record. Don't forget, cassettes hadn't been invented yet so tape players were still reel-to-reel things the size of a suitcase. And before you start laughing, there really were in-car record players during the late 1950s and 1960s. There were even players that stacked records in sequence under the dash, a bit like an old version of a CD autochanger.

To work successfully while the car was bouncing down the road, the needle required a huge weight to keep it in the groove. Tracking weights were so heavy that the needle didn't just follow the groove, it tried to cut its way through to the other side. This meant that records lasted only a few plays before they wore out, and it wasn't until the introduction of eight-track cartridges and cassettes in the 1960s that car stereo became an alternative way of listening to music without ruining your record collection.

These two tape formats didn't really fight it out like VHS and Betamax video systems did, but cassettes became the popular choice and ended up with the market all to themselves. Cartridges actually offered better sound quality, but there were problems with the endless tape system, and cassettes were more adaptable because you could record on to them.

Tapes weren't perfect, but they did give good results and everyone seemed happy enough with them until Compact Discs arrived in the 1980s. Cynics might say that CDs were invented to kick-start the stagnant home hi-fi market – nothing new had arrived on that scene for years – but there was more to CDs than that.

While there might have been a little marketing motivation behind the new format, CDs had lots going for them and, for the first time in audio playback history, you could listen to your own music without wearing it out.

About the time that CD was making a niche for itself, a couple of digital tape formats were also introduced. These were DCC and

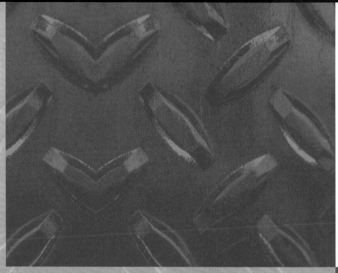

DAT and, for the purposes of this book and car audio in general, we're mentioning them only in passing.

They weren't compatible with each other because of the style of tape cassettes and tape reader systems, but they did give the opportunity to make digital copies of CDs while keeping somewhere close to the original CD quality. What they didn't offer was the sheer user-friendliness of CD, with its instant track selection and programming possibilities.

Neither format really took off. Although almost all the head unit manufacturers produced one DAT or DCC player when the formats were introduced, there are very few still knocking about today.

Nearly 20 years on, we're all used to the shiny silver disc as our preferred music storage system and now that there are writable (and re-writable) CDs, we've even got into the habit of making our own compilations again.

Technology marches on, though, and other computer-based systems are rapidly offering more ways to use and store music at home, in the car and out jogging. But we'll go into these alternatives more deeply in the next chapter. For now, let's just look at how to get what you want without buying the wrong thing.

Okay, I > want it, where do I get it?

There are plenty of places to buy your equipment these days, so you should take a bit of time deciding which outlet is going to get a large chunk of your cash.

But before we even get into what you want, let's talk about bargains. Bargains are generally thought to be good things that should be pursued whenever possible. Now, that isn't necessarily true.

A genuine bargain means being able to buy *exactly* what you want, but for less than you were expecting to pay for it. Simple as that. You walk into a shop expecting to shell out £300 for something and then find out it's gone down to £250. That's a bargain. But it isn't any of the following:

- Last year's model that isn't quite as good as you really wanted, but is cheaper than it used to be.
- A different manufacturer's equivalent that isn't exactly what you'd set your heart on, but is a few quid less.
- A much cleverer set that will possibly sound better when you've changed everything else in your system to show the improvement.
- Oh, and it's only cheaper because it's actually a factory-refurb, which means it's already gone faulty once before, but it's all sorted now. Probably.

Okay, that may be a bit cynical, but the point is this – you shouldn't be swayed into buying something that's a 'bargain' purely because the shop has a pile of them that it needs to get shot of. Of course, you should listen to someone's advice if they can offer you a genuinely better alternative to your original choice, but just be wary of anyone who simply says: 'Get one of these – they're cheaper.' The 'cheaper' one will cost you more in the long run if you end up changing it for the one you really wanted in the first place, which is a real possibility.

So where do you find out what gear is around, what it will do and what's worth buying? Well, there are numerous car styling magazines that test gear, and there are even specialist car stereo publications that go into it all a bit deeper.

The best way to find a good dealer is to go by word-of-mouth recommendations. If you keep hearing that one particular shop is particularly switched on, there's a good chance they'll see you right, too.

If no single dealer stands out from the personal recommendations, then visit a few shops yourself to see what they suggest and how they answer your searching questions when you put them on the spot. The only question a proper specialist store really won't appreciate is: 'Can you do it any cheaper?'

If you're only interested in buying something because it's cheap, don't expect a great deal of sales service, either before or after you buy. The cheap shops have to sell lots of gear quickly to stay afloat. A specialist's approach will be slightly different.

If you want to get a good system for your motor and the

person in the shop is willing to talk you through all the possibilities open to you, then it's worth paying a bit extra. So don't be tempted by the person who is prepared to knock a couple of quid off but can't answer your questions. Ask yourself this: who will be able to help out better if you get stuck when you're fitting it?

Specialist dealers should be able to spend more time getting to know what you really need. That means you should end up with a system that does exactly what you want, which is worth a small premium. Better still, if it doesn't, some specialist dealers will even swap equipment after you've bought it. That kind of service is sadly lacking at a pile-it-high, flog-it-cheap car audio shop.

Once you've found a shop you think you're going to get on with, have a good look round their demo car or some customers' cars to make sure they're on your wavelength. There's no point is asking them to help you build a Sound Pressure Level (SPL) monster if they've never done anything louder than a pair of woofers in a ready-made box, for instance. Likewise, you shouldn't expect them to tell you what will sound absolutely brilliant if all they do is fill cars with woofers and add the odd tweeter to the top of the dash.

Of course, you can always cut out the human contact altogether and buy your gear over the Internet, but this can be even more traumatic than buying your new equipment through mail-order. We've heard lots of stories about people who have ordered a stereo, only for it to take weeks to arrive, or for a different one that's *almost* what they ordered to turn up in its place. Eventually.

Watch out for little cop-out lines on the bottom of ads, too – things like 'All stock subject to availability' or 'If it isn't in stock a similar product will be offered', and any similar phrases that cover up for possible problems, such as keeping your money for a couple of months before anything's sent to you. There are reputable mail order or Internet shops around, of course, but it's important to check how confident you are before you give them that credit card number.

Generally speaking,
and making assumptions

As you read through this book, you'll notice the words 'generally' and 'probably' turn up quite a bit. That's because car audio and its related subjects are full of areas where something will work really well in one car, but not so well in another. This is normally because vehicle interiors are so different from one another and that there are too many variables to give an absolute recommendation of what will work for every car.

Take kickpanel speaker builds as an example. These can work extremely well in some cars - we know because we've heard them. The music will appear to come at you from somewhere along the bonnet – and sound as good as the day it was recorded, in some cases. But in others, your tunes will be crawling across the floor and sound completely wrong. It's all a case of knowing what works in different vehicles. It's another area where an experienced dealer comes in handy when you're asking about possible installations.

So once you've found your perfect car audio dealer, what sort of system should you go for? Well, for the purposes of this book, we're assuming your vehicle has some sort of digital head unit, four-speaker system that you want to build on. Almost any car

available since the mid-1990s has been kitted out to some degree, and by now almost all cars that left the factory with no stereo have had something fitted by a previous owner.

This means that some of the groundwork will have been done for you - there'll probably be a set of head unit wires that you can use for your new stereo, and there should be some form of radio antenna to help you pluck some choice tunes from the airwaves. But if you're going for any sort of serious audio upgrade, that will be as much as is usable.

Bearing in mind how cheap - especially compared with today's wages - car audio has become, we're also going to assume you want something that will sound decent, and go reasonably loud. If you follow a few simple guidelines, you can expand on any of the ideas we'll show you and end up with something that either sounds absolutely fabulous or gets mentally loud. It depends on whether you want to impress yourself or everyone else walking down the street.

Although we get really involved with a lot of hands-on stuff later in the book, we won't be going into anything that's too heavy and competition-biased. This is an area where things get pretty specialised and it requires up-to-date knowledge of the current rulebooks and competition formats. But we will be giving a few pointers and passing on some competition contacts, so you can investigate things further if you'd like.

We're also leaving out installation methods that require too many special tools or skills. After all, it's all very well explaining the methods of vacuum-forming ABS plastic, but if you haven't got access to a vac-forming plant, what's the point? Instead, we'll stick to the methods that almost everyone can do in their own garage with a simple toolkit.

Like a lot of very knowledgeable folk in the ICE industry, we're big believers in the KISS principle. KISS stands for Keep It Simple, Stupid, and basically means that if there is a complicated way and an easy way to achieve the same results, take the easy route every time. Keep things straightforward and you should have fewer problems and if you do get any, they should be less painful to sort.

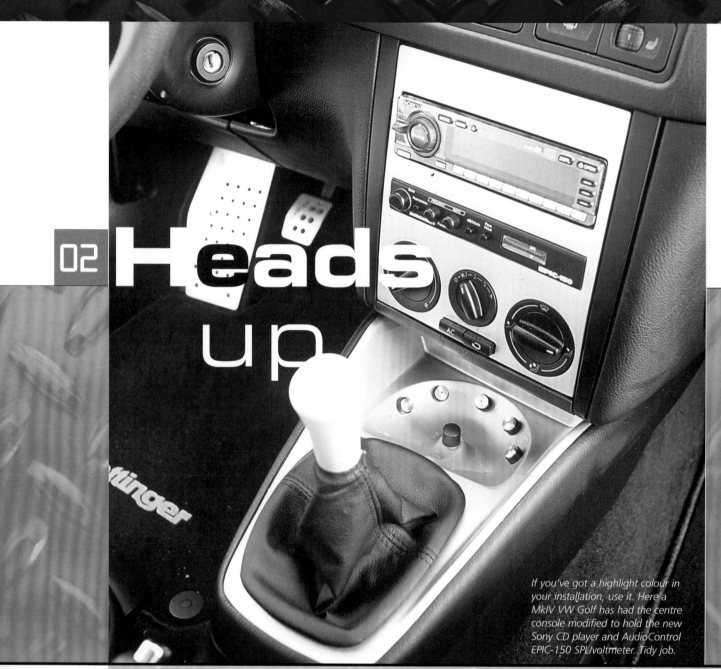

Heads up

If you've got a highlight colour in your installation, use it. Here a MkIV VW Golf has had the centre console modified to hold the new Sony CD player and AudioControl EPIC-150 SPL/voltmeter. Tidy job.

Choices, choices

Every type of system starts with some form of head unit. Whether you use cassette tapes, CDs, MiniDiscs or any of the new computer formats, your car audio system begins with a box - or boxes - of electronics that retrieves a stored or broadcast musical signal for the rest of your system to play with. It's called a head unit because it's at the head of the system. That system then reacts to the signals it receives from further up the line.

So which head unit will be good for you and your installation? That depends on what exactly you want it

to do. For instance, there's very little point in buying a radio/cassette and CD autochanger combination if you have no cassettes to speak of, or getting a MiniDisc player if you've no way of recording your own MDs at home.

This brings us back to the subject of how to find a good dealer (see Chapter 1). You really need someone who can listen to all your individual circumstances, and then point out exactly what will do the right job.

So what are the alternatives available at the moment, and what are their pros and cons? Well, we aren't going to recommend any specific pieces of kit, mainly because if you're reading this a couple of years after it was written, the models will be history. We don't want you to be laughed at by some dealers for asking about something that's been gone for a while.

By the way, if any dealers do do this, wipe the smile off their face by walking out of the shop and going

How's that for head unit security? This hand-painted cover looks like a walnut panel containing extra engine gauges.

elsewhere. Never forget that *you* are doing *them* a favour by spending your money with them, not the other way around.

Before we get into all the different music storage formats, there are a few general head unit rules worth knowing. Most important is that the quality of the head unit will define the quality of the rest of the system. This idea comes from domestic audio and has been proved right time and time again. Basically it means that the signal available on your music storage device – CD, MD, cassette or whatever – needs to be retrieved in as much detail as possible so that the rest of the system can replay it as perfectly as possible.

As an example, imagine a ropy old CD player hooked up to a fantastic amp and speaker set-up. Any crackles, distortion or polluting of the music will come straight out of the player and be amplified along with whatever music the player managed to find. Instead of glorious, high-fidelity tunes, you'll get some music and all the crackles, distortion and pollutants for good luck. Not brilliant, especially if the amps and speakers cost you so much.

On the other hand, a top-quality player will get every last bit of detail from the recording, add nothing nasty to it, and then pass it on at a decent voltage level to make the amp and speakers' job a bit easier. It's best summed up by the common computer phrase GIGO – Garbage In, Garbage Out.

If you've got a good signal to go through the rest of the system, you stand half a chance of it sounding right. If it's naff from the start, it's just going to get more naff as it gets louder. It all boils down to this: get the best head unit you can afford – within reason – and hook it up to a decent system. Then you'll be laughing.

To couple your head unit into your new system you'll need some form of non-amplified, or line-level signal output to send on to your arsenal of power amps. Almost all head units have one pre-out - as they are known - and plenty have two or three, allowing them to be used in lots of different types of installs. You can even get sets that have dedicated sub-bass outputs with their own crossover functions, too.

As for the built-in power that head units have, this can be fine to get a system going, and plenty of cars use the power in the set to run a couple of speakers when the rest of the system is externally amplified. If you want to get really decent sounds, you will need separate power amps, but choose the right head unit and it will work with you through all your system expansion.

That sorted, the next thing to do is look at the format options around at the moment.

The Alpine CDA-7878R is one of the new breed of CD players that can also handle CD-Rs filled with up to 12 hours of MP3 files. How long do you want to stay in your car at once?

The Alpine CHA-1214 only plays CDs, but it holds 12 of them, and swaps them incredibly rapidly.

Alpine's CVA-1005R shows how to get a widescreen monitor into a single dashboard slot with ease.

For MiniDisc fans who want to control a CD autochanger and get decent radio functions, there's always the Alpine MDM-7741R.

Get it **taped**

Cassette tapes are the oldest of the playback options currently available, and they've been largely overtaken for several good reasons. Cassettes still do have a few things going for them, but it seems that every new model line-up brings out an alternative that knocks another nail in their coffin.

Heads up

The cassette used to have two main advantages over its rivals. It could be recorded and re-recorded very easily, and it was very, very robust. Almost everyone has jumped into a car to find tapes covered in dust and cigarette ash cluttering up the footwell and centre console – and then watched as the owner has picked one up, blown the worst of the muck off, and stuck it in the player. It isn't the recommended way to treat them, but lots have been abused like that and still they keep on playing.

However, with the introduction of formats such as MiniDisc and CD-Rs, cassettes really are on their way out. Very well-recorded tapes, played back on a really good system, still have the ability to sound wonderful, but when you consider that actually playing a cassette degrades its performance and shortens its lifespan, you can see why other formats have passed it by.

Hindsight is a wonderful thing. When CDs first came out, the sound quality was lacking in warmth and smoothness, so good cassette tapes were pushed by hi-fi enthusiasts as the only sensible format for in-car use. Back then, CDs seemed to be simply the choice of the gadget freak who had to have everything just because it was new. Well, CD sound quality has come on so much that almost all tape systems would struggle to keep up with it now. So unless you are a real diehard tape fan, you'll probably want to look elsewhere.

A round trip

When CDs became available in the late 1980s, it seemed the best thing about them was that you could spread jam on them, clean them off in a dishwasher and they'd play as well as if they'd never been gooed up. At least, that was the received wisdom of television programmes.

The amazing thing about CDs isn't how they work but the fact that they work at all. The music signal is digitally encoded as a series of small 'pits' in the reflective surface of the disc and strung out in a single line like a groove on a record. Unlike records, though, CDs play from the middle outwards, and they spin much faster.

Probably the most sophisticated head unit in the world? Alpine want you to think so. The CDA-7990R is part of their F#1 Status range that is super-expensive, and mega-specced.

Not strictly a head unit, the PXA-H900 belongs with the CDA-7990R and performs so much digital processing it's faster than a well-specced desktop computer.

Tired of going into the boot to change CDs in your autochanger? Nakamichi's MB-100 stores six discs internally, so they're always at your fingertips. The outboard Digital/Analogue Converter (DAC) is top class.

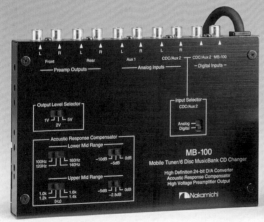

Some people go a bit over the top when they change their dash to put a new head unit in. This is a Ford Cougar that's been treated to a full set of Dakota Digital gauges along with its new CD player.

Not only has the Blaupunkt Los Angeles MP71 got an MP3-compatible CD drive, it also has a three-band equaliser on board to compensate for troublesome vehicle acoustics.

The microscopic size of the bits of information and the speed at which they're read are just mind-blowing. To give you an idea of scale, if a CD was the size of the Coliseum in Rome, one pit in the 'groove' would be about the size of a match head. As for speed, the sampling rate of a CD is 44.1 kiloHertz, meaning those pits are read at a speed of 44,100 times per second.

What the gimmick-mongers didn't point out was that the early discs, and the early disc players, left a lot to be desired in sound quality. Plenty of people reckoned they'd never heard anything so clean and wonderful in their lives, but this was more a reflection of how awful their existing music system was rather than how good the new CD player was. Things have changed a bit since then…

Now CDs are widely regarded as the best-sounding format – discounting vinyl LPs, which don't really get much of a look-in in car stereo circles – and there are new mastering and recording techniques designed to capture on CD even more detail and information from the original performance.

The Fusion fch-3000 six-disc changer can be hooked up to any of Fusion's head units, but with the fch-m FM modulator, it can be added to any OE head unit, too.

Just about the only thing those naff TV programmes got right at CD's birth was their robustness. They can be treated with fairly heavy hand and still do their job. But once they get deeply or widely scratched, they'll skip and stick like a rap sample. And if they do that, they're only fit for the bin. But just check first that the skipping isn't being caused by a jammy fingerprint, which can easily be wiped off…

As CDs' and CD players' general sound quality has increased, CD player costs have plummeted. An early Pioneer in-car CD player used to sell for £500. It had a separate power supply box that was bigger than the in-dash player itself. The CD player needed to be interfaced to another head unit because it didn't have any in-built volume or tone controls, or amplification. In fact, it had no other source functions at all, and its anti-skip isolation system was a bit rudimentary.

Now, you can get a CD player with a very sophisticated radio, controls for a separate CD autochanger, in-built hi-power amplification and loads more stuff for less than a third of that figure. Oh, it'll also be a one-box installation that can be fitted to some cars in less than a minute, and it'll never skip unless the car's involved in a major collision.

But CDs aren't perfect. Until recently, you couldn't record on to them, and although you can burn your own discs on your PC or domestic CD player, some in-car players can't read them. It seems that every time someone figures out a way round a problem, another one comes up to catch them out again.

CD-Rs and CD-RWs are also a bit variable for sound quality. Depending on the sampling rate at which they were recorded, they can sound as good as the original disc they were copied from, or they can sound very harsh, compressed and pretty unpleasant.

Even so, CDs' problems are fairly minor. They are probably the best-sounding format you can have in a car today – and will be for the near future.

Minimus discimus

The diminutive MiniDisc is a wonderful device that can be recorded on to at home, and then played back in any MD player without the non-compatibility worries of some CD-Rs. These new discs are just so small that personal MD players

Blaupunkt are proud of their Woodstock DAB 52 because it is the first unit in the world to combine a DAB tuner and an MP3 CD drive in one chassis.

The Fusion fch-m FM modulator converts the signal from the fch-3000 into a radio signal that any head unit can tune into.

>

This BMW
never came
from the
factory with a
radio display in
the instrument
panel. This has
been added by
a very clever
audio installer.

are even smaller than personal cassette players. In-car ones are often multiplayers that can sit in a standard dash opening and take three or four discs.

Their biggest advantage – apart from their size – is that the easily damaged disc is hidden away inside a sleeve that protects it from almost everything. That means they can be treated as roughly as an old cassette without affecting their playback ability. It's just that the playback ability can be a bit of a question mark.

To get all that wonderful music to fit on to such a tiny disc, the audio signal has to be very heavily compressed. This compression system is the root of the problem. The first versions fitted plenty of music on the disc, but lost most of the quality while doing it. Even now, with some major leaps forward in the technology,

The Clarion MXZ718R combines the convenience of a MiniDisc player with an ultra-clever DAB tuner for top-notch radio performance.

If your dash can stand the strain, a double-DIN unit like Clarion's ADX5655Rz has a CD player, a cassette player, and an RDS tuner all in one box.

anyone who has a MiniDisc and CD system can usually tell the difference between the two formats. Like CDs, though, there are constant efforts to improve the MD's sound quality, so this will become less of an issue as the format progresses.

The latest twist to MiniDisc is the MD-LP, which means that a normal 80-minute MD can provide up to five hours of music.

Testing, testing, MP3

The ability to turn music into MP3 files has created quite a stir in the home computer and hi-fi markets and it has begun to catch on for in-car use, too. While most people get hung up on ways of getting free MP3 music over the Internet, the main advantage of MP3 encoding for in-car use is that you can fit oodles of music on one CD-R, hard drive or memory chip. It could

The Panasonic CQ-DRX900N has the novelty of a centre-channel speaker built into the front of the unit to help the performance of its onboard DSP section.

As well as its CD player and RDS tuner capability, the Panasonic CQ-SRX7000 also plays files stored on an SD memory card that can be inserted below the CD slot. One hour of music on something the size of a postage stamp, anyone?

Put a Panasonic CQ-RD115 radio cassette and a CX-DP88 together and you've got three choices of music on the move.

be stuff you already own or have borrowed from an outside source. But whatever it is, you can have several hours of it and take up very little space in your motor.

The speed with which the technology is moving means that, as we put this book together, there are already other computer-based formats arriving on the scene. At the moment, it's impossible to say with any certainty which one will become dominant, but for now all we know is that there are a lot of people going after the same market. If you are a real fan of technology and have to have the latest format, be prepared to lose a few quid as things come and go.

If you just want to be able to use MP3 files as your preferred music medium, get hold of one of the new CD players that can read MP3-encoded discs, and use your home computer to burn your downloaded and existing music. You should end up with about 12 hours of music on each disc, and you'll be able to play your existing CDs as well. We reckon that's probably the best bet at the moment, but we might well have to rewrite this section in a couple of years. It's impossible to say right now.

Fusion's ftd-1000 radio cassette player can also drive their six-disc changer, and has two pre-outs for system expansion.

Ethereal signals

If you were expecting the definitive guide to how radio works, what transmitters do and how a receiver translates the signal it picks up into one you can listen to, then you've come to the wrong place. The fundamentals of radio theory have been covered in vast depth by numerous other publications, so we're concentrating on pointing out a few useful features to look for on your new head unit as well as a couple of good ideas about aerials.

On the majority of new head units, which combine a radio with something else, the radio will almost certainly be an RDS unit. We've had a look through numerous manufacturer catalogues and the only differences between their radio sections seem to be the number of RDS features rather than whether or not they have RDS at all.

So what's RDS? Well the Radio Data System basically uses a method of attaching extra information to the radio signal in such a way that your stereo can decode it and use it to perform numerous other useful functions. Functions such as Alternative Frequency, Traffic Information, Programme Type and RDS Regional make listening to radio a much simpler pastime than when you had to hunt up and down the dial to try to find a station you recognised as you hurtled along.

For instance, RDS sets can retune themselves to the same radio programme as alternative frequencies become available as you drive along. Also, they can break into your non-radio playback – or your national radio station – and deliver a local radio station broadcast about traffic news for the area you are driving through. It might save you from sitting in a traffic jam for hours.

If you drive out of signal range for one station, they can even find you another radio station similar to it. It's a wonderful system and almost every head unit has it.

The only really new thing happening in radio at the moment

is DAB. Digital Audio Broadcasting is a new format that offers near-CD quality sound, more stations, additional radio and data services, easier tuning and interference-free reception, as well as extra information in the form of graphics or text.

All this comes into the car stereo through a stubby antenna that looks like a shorter version of a regular aerial, but a separate DAB tuner box is needed for most installations. In Panasonic's version, for instance, a DAB tuner is added alongside a CD changer through a dual-changer interface, allowing the head unit to control both the changer and the DAB box.

If you aren't that bothered about this new way of getting radio into your car now, you soon will be. DAB will be taking over from FM in the next few years, and FM will be handed over to communications systems instead. That means you'll have to get with the programme whether you want to or not. This is a little way ahead at the moment, but if you've had this book for a while, don't say we didn't warn you.

Pioneer's entry into the DAB-tuner market is the DEH-P90DAB, which also has a very funky display to keep your passenger entertained if the road gets too boring. The Pioneer remote control attaches to the steering wheel rim so that you have thumb control of your stereo.

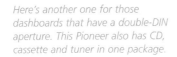
Here's another one for those dashboards that have a double-DIN aperture. This Pioneer also has CD, cassette and tuner in one package.

Added into a Panasonic system with a multi-changer adapter, this CY-DAB2000 unit gives a non-DAB head unit the chance to pick up the new radio format.

Magic wands

If you want a radio to work at all, it must have an aerial. What form that aerial takes is where the variation starts, and if you look down a line of parked cars, you'll probably see most types. Straightforward telescopic wing-mounted aerials have been the most common type for a long time, and a good quality one will do a sterling job of plucking the signal from the air. Motorised telescopic antennas do just about the same job, but they have the added convenience of appearing and disappearing when required, which makes the vandal's job harder.

Roof aerials are also popular and a good one is probably the best form of antenna for reception. These aerials are split between long and short masted, amplified and non-amplified, and front or rear mounted, but they all have similar advantages. Being fitted to a good ground plane – that means the whole of the roof panel – helps them to receive a better signal than an aerial fitted lower on

the car, on a smaller area of metal. Their anti-vandal rating is pretty good, too, because a lot of the little hooligans can't reach far enough across a roof to try to snap them off or bend them.

The heated rear window element antenna is a favourite of car manufacturers. It's very stealthy, impossible to vandalise apart from putting a brick through the glass, and you can't accidentally leave it up when you drive through a car wash. Although its performance doesn't quite hold up to that of a decent roof or wing antenna, the lack of hole in the vehicle and the anti-vandal aspect both count in its favour.

We're assuming your car has an aerial as part of the factory stereo provision, but if you do need to fit one, you should be talking to your car audio specialist. They'll be able to tell you what kind of antenna works best on your car, and what will fit.

In a lot of cases, you'll just want to replace the original item with one that uses the same hole rather drill another. Just make sure you go for a good quality aerial that will capture as much signal as possible and help to keep interference at bay.

The most likely thing you'll come up against with fitting new equipment is that the aerial socket on your new head unit and the plug on the aerial lead will be different. While many sets come with a common aerial adapter plug, you might need something a bit more sophisticated, such as an adapter that allows your head unit to power the aerial's built-in signal amplifier. Again, your dealer should have that sort of info and be able to supply the correct widget to get your radio talking to your aerial.

It's worth being aware that some factory-fitted screen aerials can be drastically expensive to repair if they go faulty. For instance, some Ford Escorts were fitted with rear screen aerials and the aerial lead was fed into the hatch through a rubber grommet. After a few years of opening and closing the hatch, the cable used to fail because it was being constantly flexed. The cost of rewiring the aerial was a bit mad, so the best bet was to fit a front-mounted roof aerial instead.

If you have any aerial problems, try an ICE specialist before you try the vehicle's main dealer. A good audio store should have come across the problem before and have a sensible solution. Going down the factory route will probably cost a load more.

Do you want five hours of music from one MiniDisc? Then the Sony MDX-CA680 is for you. With its MDLP facility, you can play specially-recorded MDs for ages.

With due process

Once a head unit has injected the signal into a system, it can go straight on to one or more amplifiers, and from there it can bounce out of your speakers. It *can*, but in many systems it has to be tweaked a bit by some form of signal processor first.

This could be something as simple as an electronic low-pass filter built into an amplifier. Or it could be as complicated as a line driver, followed by twin 30-band equalisers, multi-channel active filtering and a parametric bass-synthesising processor, before there's even a sniff of the amplification. On top of these items,

With a 14-band equaliser, BBE-effect circuitry - which is supposed to enhance the apparent spaciousness of the sound - and surround sound processing, the Alpine ERA-G320 equaliser can keep a knob-twiddler happy for weeks.

many installations are being kitted out with DSP and AV processors that might appear to be more useful in a cinema.

So what are these anonymous black boxes, what do they do exactly and why do we need them at all? Some systems seem to get by perfectly well without them, so what makes them essential for others? Well, there are lots of reasons for using any or all of these devices, so let's go through a few to see if you need them.

Keep on **driving**

The line driver is a signal doodad that has grown in popularity over the past few years. It's probably simplest to think it as a small amplifier. It boosts the size of signal coming from a head unit up to a much higher level so that the main system amplifier has an easier job to do.

By lifting the signal level at the head unit, there is less chance for interference to bleed into the music before it travels the length of the car and reaches the amp rack. The fatter signal is also more dynamic and has more life to it, so the music produced by the

The Phoenix Gold Pro Line Driver lifts a head unit's line-level output up to a maximum of eight volts, more than enough to keep the music dynamic, lively and interference-free.

system has more bounce and energy to it.

The final benefit is that the line driver can help to quieten the rest of the system and get rid of background hiss. This hiss, often called floor noise, is the sound of the electronics in the system processing and amplifying the input signal into something that the speakers can deal with. In simple terms, by raising the voltage level of the music signal, there's less room for hiss to be reproduced, which lowers the system's overall noise floor.

As we'll see when we get on to setting a system's gain structure – which means setting up the system levels – gain should be introduced in the quietest component in the system, and not in the noisiest. So a line driver allows a nice dynamic signal to be replayed without needing to turn up the gain on the amplifier, which is often a noisier component than anything else that comes before it.

Divide and conquer

The most widely used electronic processor in car audio is the active crossover. Many amplified installations have them, but rather than being a separate unit they are very often built into the amplifier itself. This makes for easier system wiring and means there are fewer boxes to fit in. But whether the active crossovers are built in or stand alone, they do much the same thing.

A crossover is a device that splits up the incoming frequency into two or more chunks for use by other parts of the system. A passive crossover – made up from a combination of capacitors and coils – is generally supplied with a speaker component kit, and it's fitted after the amp but before the speakers.

Apart from a couple of output level adjustments, most passives don't have any tweakable controls. We'll look at these in a bit more detail in the speaker section.

The difference between a passive and an active crossover is that the active unit comes before the amplification and can often be tweaked in several ways. They can usually be adjusted to allow fine tuning of the point where the signal splits occur, and of the level of each of the outputs. Frequency adjustments can either be done with potentiometers that are tweaked with a screwdriver or thumbnail, or by the less convenient – but ultimately more accurate – plug-in resistor packs.

The products that use potentiometers – or pots for short – are more easily tweaked and the results are easier to spot. Plug-in resistor packs aren't as user-friendly but they have two main

The Alpine ERE-G180 equaliser is a bit more basic than its electronic brother, but you can still tweak your sound with its 11 EQ bands and built-in sub-bass crossover.

With due process

advantages – they can't be moved accidentally and they can't alter through vibration. Once a 90Hz resistor pack is fitted into an active's socket, that crossover point will remain at 90Hz until a pack with a different value is fitted in its place.

The choice between pots or packs should be determined by the other crossover's features as well as dealer back-up. You should also consider how much tweaking you might want to do. If you just want to listen to the system as it comes from the shop, you have less need for the instant tweakability of something that's fitted with pots.

On the other hand, if you want to try different settings to have a go at improving your system, being able to twist a pot might be very useful. Should you want the accuracy of a resistor pack-type crossover but fancy having a play with your system's settings, make sure your dealer carries a full range of other packs. Without them, you can't chop and change things around until you're happy.

The PXA-H510 signal processor is a Dolby Digital and Dolby Pro-Logic device that can bring movies to life. Full 5.1 digital processing lets it turn your system into a cinema on wheels, if the rest of your gear is up to it...

The simplest active crossover is a high- or low-pass filter, which extracts the part of the signal needed by the amplifier stage and discards the rest. This type is almost exclusively built in to an amp and is used to change it from full-range operation to dedicated sub-bass or higher-frequency use.

Filter tips

As the name implies, low-pass or high-pass filters let only the part of the frequency bandwidth they need through the filter. So if a low-pass filter is set to 80Hz, everything below 80Hz will pass through but the rest will die off. Conversely, a 125Hz high-pass will suffocate everything below 125Hz, allowing the rest of the music through to be beefed up in the amp.

Many amps now have clever crossover stages built-in, and this sophistication isn't always dependent on how many channels the amplifier can deal with internally. There are quite a few two-channel amps with a crossover that allows one part of the audio to be used by its own circuitry while sending the remaining signal through a set of output sockets so that it can be used in another amp or processor. In some multi-channel amplifiers, the crossover functions can get even more complicated.

Outboard active crossovers are often more sophisticated than the built-ins, with two-way, three-way and even four-way units available for systems that require a large amount of slicing and dicing of the audio signal. As with everything else in car audio, though, there are pros and cons with this amount of chopping, so your choice should be based on the type of system you want to install and what will work well in your vehicle.

Many great-sounding installations use a simple two-way active crossover that just splits off the sub bass for separate amplification and leaves the rest of the audio to be dealt with by another amp. This arrangement often gives the biggest improvement over a passively filtered system that's being run by a single amp – and there are good reasons for this.

In a single-amp system that uses a combination of capacitors and coils to split passively the correct signal to each of the speakers, the performance of the front or satellite speakers can often be corrupted by the sub-bass requirements. Here's why.

Imagine a music track with a pounding bass line that really gets the sub woofer moving. When the amp has to deal with making that sub thump, the power available for the front speakers can often dip in time with the bass pulse. This problem is made worse when the volume is turned up and the bass signal gets bigger. More voltage is sapped by the sub signal and the rest of the music suffers because the amp has run out of reserves to keep the front speakers kicking, too.

Now think about the same track going through an active crossover and on to two separate amps. The thumping bass line is still there, and the sub-bass amp passes that power on to the sub woofer. The difference is that the other amp is unaffected by the high-power bass, and still has plenty of juice to run the satellites and allow them to keep up with the subs, almost regardless of how far the wick is turned up.

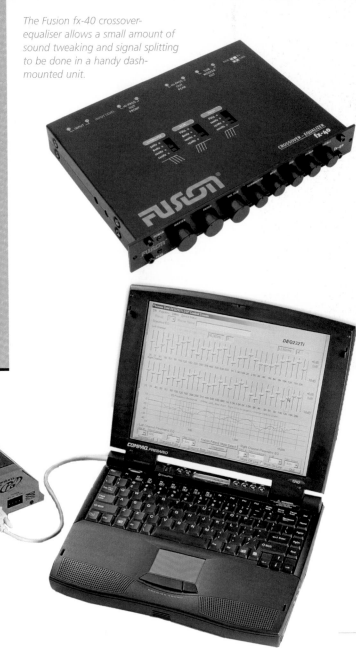

The Fusion fx-40 crossover-equaliser allows a small amount of sound tweaking and signal splitting to be done in a handy dash-mounted unit.

State-of-the-art computer-controlled equalisation is here. The Phoenix Gold DEQ232Ti doesn't look like much, but it can offer a good system tuner masses of flexibility for setting up a car audio system.

Because the amps are adjustable separately, the level of sub or fronts can be tweaked independently of the other, giving more control of the final sound. It's a big improvement over a passive system.

With this big a system to control, it's no surprise to see two 30-band equalisers looking after the tweaking in this vehicle.

Three-way split

Moving up from the simple two-way active split you get – unsurprisingly – to three-way. This is normally where the front mid-range and tweeter speakers are run by separate channels of amplification, and the frequency split is done by another active crossover. In the two-way active we've just looked at, the front speakers would be split by their dedicated passive filters, so this three-way set-up is the next logical step.

By going for a three-way active crossover, the front end of

system is more controllable. Now the tweeters and mid ranges can be adjusted separately from each other, and if the crossover has pots rather than plug-in resistors, the actual crossover points can be tweaked as you listen and search for the best settings. This extra adjustability can be very useful for systems where the speaker position is less than ideal, or simply because of personal preference.

But having given with one hand, the laws of car audio are about to take away with the other. By being more tweakable, there are also more chances to get the sound wrong. You could end up with expensive equipment in your car that just doesn't do it

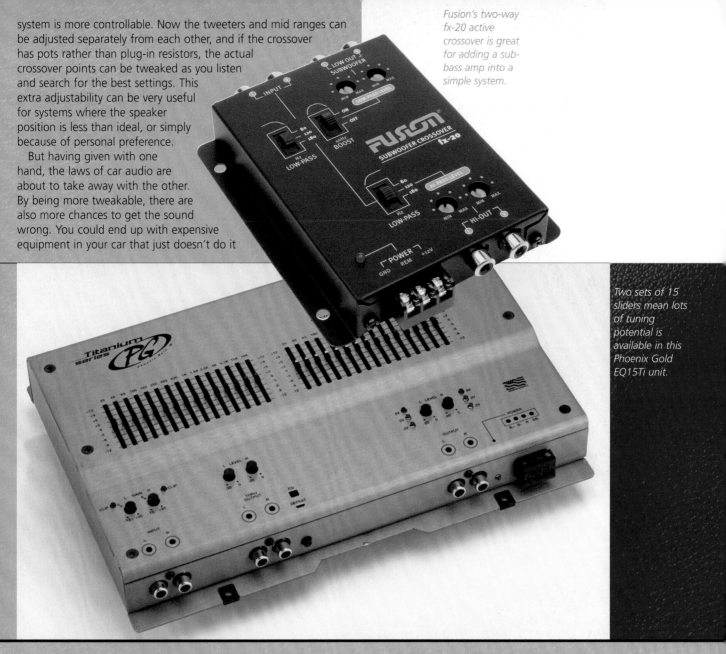

Fusion's two-way fx-20 active crossover is great for adding a sub-bass amp into a simple system.

Two sets of 15 sliders mean lots of tuning potential is available in this Phoenix Gold EQ15Ti unit.

for you because it doesn't sound too clever. We've heard plenty of systems like that.

There's another thing that many people miss when they go fully active – as it's known – on a speaker system. You almost always throw away the dedicated passive crossover that came with the mids and tweets. This item often does more than just sort out the crossover point. In a lot of these passive networks, there are compensation filters that smooth out the sound each speaker produces. Get rid of these passives with their equalising effect and you might have more adjustment of speaker levels and crossover points, but you could end up with strange, audible 'spikes' in the music.

Also, a three-way active set-up is a more expensive proposition. You need at least five channels of discreet amplification – one for sub, two for mids and two for tweets – and it will need to be balanced. This is where your friendly dealer comes in handy.

You should be able to get some good advice about which amps work well together, so the components are nicely balanced before the tweaking begins. There's no point spending hours searching for a pukka setting when the goodies you've fitted just won't work that well together, regardless of the way they're tuned.

Four armed

If the three-way system isn't enough, you can go all out for a four-way set-up. This gives you sub bass for the low rumble, separate mid bass for some real kick, and then mid range and treble to fill in the rest of the picture. But if there were careful considerations with using a three-way system, there are even more when going to four-way.

How's that for a neat installation position for a pair of 30-band equalisers? Mounted under one top plate, the two Zapco equalisers can be twiddled by the passenger as the system is being set up.

Slippery slopes

Most car stereo specialists – even those who manufacture and sell three-way speaker sets to go with a separate sub woofer – will admit that there can be problems in using and setting up a three-way speaker array in a car. This is made even more challenging when using them in an active system, so be warned.

You could be chasing a perfect set-up that is unobtainable with so many speakers and amp channels. For more details about three-way front-end problems, turn to the speaker section.

Before we leave the subject of active crossovers, it's worth mentioning the crossover slope. Once you start looking at their specs, you'll see figures mentioned like 6dB/octave, 12dB/octave, 18dB/octave and even 24dB/octave. These also apply to passive networks. But what do these figures mean and, more important, what's an octave?

Put simply, an octave is a doubling or halving of any frequency. One octave higher than 100Hz is 200Hz, one octave lower than 5000Hz is 2500Hz. The accepted bandwidth of human hearing is from 20Hz to 20,000Hz, so we can hear a range of ten octaves.

The slope of the crossover is the rate at which it cuts off those unwanted frequencies that shouldn't be passed on to the amplifier or speakers. In some applications a very mild slope – 6dB per octave – is useful to allow one speaker to blend in to the sound coming from the other one it's working with. This can be something like a mid-range driver mounted low in a door that needs to blend into a tweeter mounted higher in the cabin.

On the other hand, a very steep slope can be used to stop a speaker being damaged by trying to reproduce a range beyond its design limits. This might happen if a speaker designer wants to protect a tweeter, but also to run it down to a lower treble frequency than might normally be used. By using something like a 24dB/octave filter, the output below the chosen crossover point falls away rapidly.

Another reason for using a steep slope can be found at the opposite end of the spectrum – a subsonic filter. This allows a sub woofer to play down to a very low frequency – around 20-30Hz – but then it cuts the signal very rapidly below that. When adjusted correctly, a subsonic filter stops the amplifier wasting energy trying to recreate very low notes that might not be heard. If it's set up poorly, it actually gets in the way of the very necessary sub-bass output and pulls the foundation out from under the music.

Some active crossovers have adjustable slopes as well as frequency and level, so a skilled system tuner has plenty of choices to get the best blend between all the rest of the componentry fitted in the car.

This MacAudio passive crossover is unusual because you can use two separate channels of amplification into it rather than one. This can help to keep the speakers sounding the way they should without needing extra equalisation.

Some are **more equal** than others

An equaliser is another piece of signal processing equipment often seen in car audio systems. Equalisers range from the small amplified units found on market stalls right up to computer-controlled monsters. One costs less than a decent takeaway meal, the other more than many people's cars.

We mention the little amplified graphic equalisers because everyone's seen them and probably played with one at some point – and they do have their uses. If you have an old radio/cassette that produces only minimal power – a factory-fitted 2x7watts or something like that – you can give it a bit of a boost by fitting a cheap equaliser. You'll only lift the power output to something like 2x25watts, but the extra tone control will help you to get a bit more thump and sparkle from your tunes.

The reason that these units, and some of their more expensive cousins, are called graphic equalisers comes from the way they are adjusted. These equalisers use a bank – or banks in the more sophisticated stereo EQs – of sliders to tweak the different sections of the audio spectrum.

The Phoenix Gold BassCube can help you tweak your sub-bass, or blow your windows out. It's your choice.

A market-stall hero might have only five or seven sliders spread equally from bass to treble, but a top-flight unit will have 30 sliders and a few will even have 30 for each channel. Once they're adjusted, the sliders form a graphic representation of the equalisation curve that's been applied to the music. Easy.

Now that we have some pretty high-powered head units available, the need for the cheap-and-cheerful version has dwindled quite a bit, so let's leave it behind. A good head unit will produce as much or more power than the equaliser/booster could manage anyway, so if you need extra tunability, do it with a decent piece of kit.

In a reasonable quality system, an equaliser needs to be half-decent or it will do more harm than good. While it will add a lot of adjustability, it could easily add too much noise and degrade the signal flowing through it, spoiling the final product. It also needs to be set up properly to get the full benefit. There are many dealers out there who sell equalisers, but when it comes to doing a decent job of setting them up, there aren't that many who can cope. Just make sure you can hear the full benefit from the kit *before* you buy it, eh?

The **low-down** on low down

The bass signal processor is one of the latest additions to the tweakable-electronics market. Although there are a few different types, they all set out to make the lowest octaves bigger and better. With a decent one that's been set-up well, and a few kilowatts of bass power kicking your car apart, you'll be worrying cashpoint alarms when you drive by.

There are a couple of reasons for using a bass processor, but the main one is to get more low-end output. They are useful to the sound quality enthusiast as well, giving an extra level of control of the system's low-end. But most people buy them to make things shake more.

The AC300 signal processor is Panasonic's answer to the in-car-cinema need for Dolby surround-sound processing, and it even has a small amp built-in to power a centre speaker.

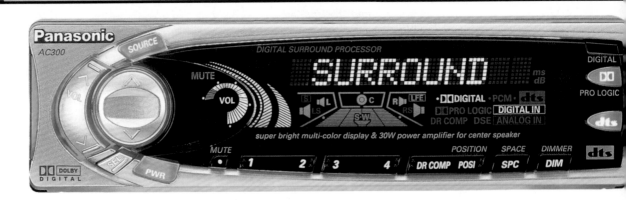

Something like Phoenix Gold's BassCube can not only add more thump to the overall sound, it can also be used to protect a sub woofer. When correctly set up, the BassCube does this by preventing the woofer from running into troublesome distortion or, if the woofer is used in a vented enclosure, stop it going below the tuned frequency of the box and doing itself a serious mischief.

The BassCube and similar processors can also be used to increase the bass output at the resonant frequency of the vehicle's interior, but that's more for the ground pounders who want to make some serious noise and rattle windows wherever they drive. For the rest of us, it's an interesting product that can be used to show off just how hard our systems can kick, every now and again…

DSP:
Dodgy signal pollution **or** digital signal perfection?

DSP units – short for Digital Signal Processor – have been around in the car audio world for a while now, and they get more sophisticated every year. Whether or not they are a good thing depends on what they are designed to do and how they are used in the system.

Early units had the gimmicky ability to make anything that went through them sound like it was in one of several different venues. By adding strange echo effects, you could end up with your favourite band playing in a stadium, a church, or a jazz club. It could be interesting, but once you'd played around with the settings and listened to Slipknot in a jazz club or the evening news read from a stadium, it seldom got much use.

A lot of units offered the saviour to all in-car problems - time alignment. Well, they thought it was the saviour, but there were a few small niggles that couldn't be got around digitally, so they didn't catch on the way most manufacturers would have liked.

Time alignment is a method of 'moving' one or more speakers by delaying the sound they produce by a tiny amount so that their musical output arrives at the listener at the same time as the music coming from a speaker that's physically further away. The idea is that you can compensate for the usual in-car problem that some speakers will be nearer than others to the listener, and therefore they will dominate the way the listener picks up the sound.

The idea sounds fantastic, but the whole thing falls a bit flat because it means optimising the sound system to one person – the driver. Now, if you're Billy NoMates, the driver and you never take passengers who listen to music, who cares that the system sounds good to you and you alone? But what if you do have listeners in the other seats occasionally? What are they going to hear? In a lot of time-aligned cars, the passenger will think that all the sound is coming at them from an air vent on their side of the dash. It's often not very nice to listen to.

It seems that the best way to get around this is to fit both left and right front speakers well away from the listeners, so that neither side dominates the sound stage. Then there's no need for the electronic jiggery pokery that will affect one side of the car badly.

We have you surrounded

Now that we have in-car cinema systems, it seems only right that we have the surround-sound processing to go with them. Once mobile DVD players became available, that digitally encoded, multi-channel soundtrack was just waiting to be used in all its glory. And done properly in a car, it's mind-blowing.

Like domestic systems, in-car surround sound can be based on most of the proprietary encoding systems, with Dolby Digital, DTS and Dolby Pro-Logic being among the best known. To get the best from the processing power built into the surround-sound decoders, the rest of the system has to be designed differently from a regular car audio system. But when it's done well, it's worth the extra effort – and cash.

The main difference is that all six amplification and speaker channels are needed to do the job properly. As well as front right and left, there's a centre speaker, left and right rear effects channels, and a separate sub woofer channel, too. In a lot of cases, this is three channels more than would usually be fitted in a car, and in almost all vehicles, the centre channel will be absolutely new.

Going the whole hog on a surround-sound system will be pretty expensive for the next few years, so you really have to ask yourself how much you need something like that. If you can't do without it, get ready for a cramping pain in the wallet – and a seriously widescreen grin whenever you play movies like *The Matrix*. Then it'll all be worthwhile.

If you run out of room to install your ICE gear, don't forget to use your ingenuity. You can always find a bit of space somewhere to fit that last piece of gear, like this equaliser in a seat back.

Amplifiers

Obviously the owner of this Honda Civic doesn't do the grocery shopping...

www.mtxaudio.com

If the head unit is the brains of the audio system, amplifiers are the heart. They take the low-level audio signal from the brain and get it pumping through the cables and speakers, which in turn belt it out into your car. In a similar way to speakers, a lot of junk is talked about amplifiers, so let's try and cut through the rubbish and see what they're really made of.

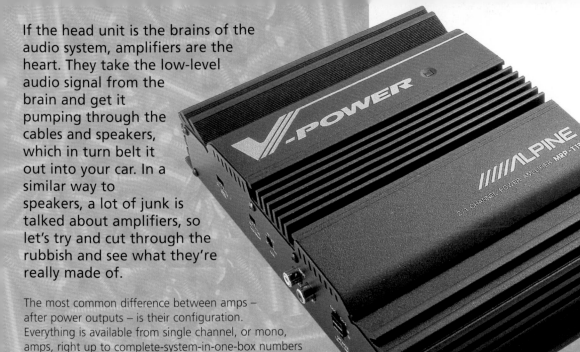

The MRP-T130 from Alpine can run a full system from one box. Simultaneous stereo/mono operation, built-in crossover, and a bass boost circuit are all available from this entry-level unit.

The most common difference between amps – after power outputs – is their configuration. Everything is available from single channel, or mono, amps, right up to complete-system-in-one-box numbers that run seven or eight channels. But probably the most commonly available and widely used are the more simple two- and four-channel amps.

These offer a sensible amount of features and often have some flexibility in how they can be used. With a bit of careful planning, the right amp can be used in different ways in numerous system designs as you expand your install, which is far better than having to trade it in.

Class acts

As well as various channel configurations, there are also different types of amplifier circuitry. These are denoted by calling the amp either Class A, Class B, Class AB, or Class D. These classes refer to the different methods used to amplify the audio signal. Without getting too bogged down in the technicalities, here are a few pointers to how each works.

Class A is said to be the most inefficient but best-sounding amplifier design around, and quite a few have been made for in-car use. They are often fairly low-power designs, but they still gulp lots of current and produce plenty of heat. Devotees of Class A design wouldn't use anything else, and reckon they could hear the difference between As and Bs blindfolded.

Class B amplifiers are much more efficient than Class A units, but there are potential problems with distortion of the audio signal caused by their circuit design. Much work has gone into minimising this, and they are so popular in car audio that you'd have to agree it probably isn't a major issue any more.

Class AB amps work as a Class A design at low levels, and then switch over to Class B as the wick is turned up. By combining

With a bridged power output of 900watts the Alpine MRV-1507 is a bit of a monster, and it has a built-in cooling fan to stop it getting too hot and bothered.

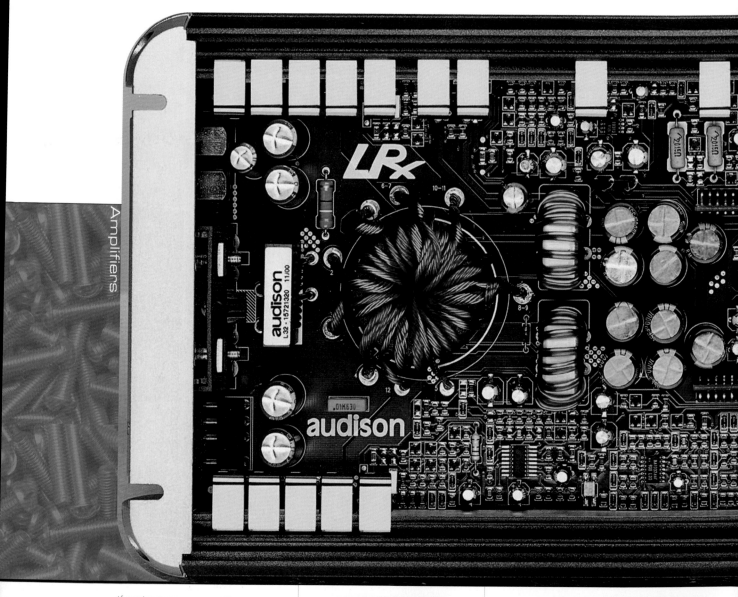

If you've ever wondered what went into a decent amplifier, look at this Audison and be amazed at how everything is packed in.

These two and four-channel MTX Thunder amps look good and sound great, and can both run systems that can be expanded using their in-built crossovers.

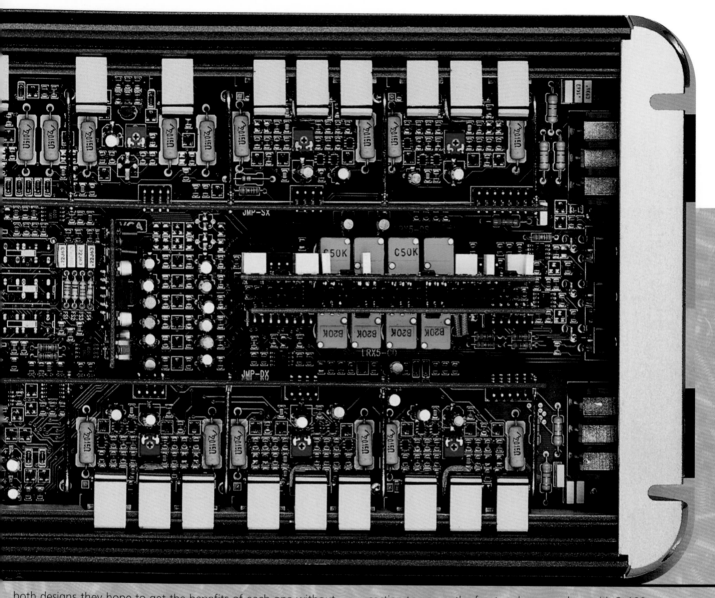

both designs they hope to get the benefits of each one without taking on the problems of either. Again, they are very popular in car audio circles and have many useful features.

Class D amplifiers are often incorrectly known as digital amps, and the way they reproduce and amplify their input signal is completely different from anything in Class A, B, or AB. They are much more efficient than these designs but they also have their own little foibles.

The main sticking point with Class D operation has always been the distortion added to the musical signal, and it is really noticeable through the mid and high frequencies. Class D amps have found a useful niche as bass amps, because the distortion element doesn't affect the bass signal. This means there are quite a few Class D bass amps available that use less current and less space than usual for a Class A or B amplifier of similar wattage.

Some car audio manufacturers make hybrid amps that combine the best features from each class design in one case. As an example, JL Audio's 500/5 amp uses a Class AB four-channel

section to power the front and rear speakers with 2x100 watts and 2x25 watts respectively, and then uses a Class D 1x250 watts section for the sub woofer. A very neat one-box solution.

If that wasn't enough to take in, a lot of amps have other tricks up their heatsinks. One of the most useful is the built-in crossover, which was described in more detail in Chapter 3 of this book. A good crossover section can happily run a decent system without the need for any other boxes of electronics and can be adjustable enough to use the amp in different ways.

Another useful trick is an amp's ability to be 'bridged'. This term means that a stereo pair of channels can be used to drive one speaker load, increasing the power output available to that speaker. In fact, so many amps can do this these days that you'll struggle to find one that doesn't – unless it's a real cheapy that isn't really worth sticking in a car anyway.

Most multi-channel amps can be bridged up in the same way. For instance, a four-channel unit can be configured either to run

Audison's solution to a system-in-one-box is this six-channel offering.

four full-range speakers or to have one pair of channels bridged to drive a sub while the other two do the front speakers. Alternatively, both pairs of channels can be joined to drive one speaker each.

The next step up from this is simultaneous bridged mono/stereo, often known as tri-mode. This is very useful for getting a full system up and running on one amp. As the phrase suggests, it means that a stereo amplifier can be wired up to a pair of front speakers and be bridged into a sub woofer at the same time. Some form of passive crossover network is required after the amplifier to sort out which frequencies go to which speakers, but it means that a single amp can run the whole system so long as the impedance doesn't drop too low.

Ah yes, impedance. Impedance is measured in ohms and is a measurement of electrical resistance. When applied to a speaker, it shows how easy or difficult it's going to be to drive that speaker. In basic terms, as impedance drops, the load becomes more difficult to drive, so the amplifier has to produce more power.

As a general rule, most car speakers are four-ohm drivers, but different wiring schemes can increase or decrease the load the amplifier has to deal with. Each halving or doubling of impedance usually has the opposite effect on the power output. For instance, if a 100watt amp is driving a four-ohm load, a two-ohm load would see 200watts, and so on. This is only a general rule, of course, and some amps won't play ball when the impedance drops too far. Follow the guidance on the box if you're unsure what your kit can manage.

As long as the amp can handle the load and there's enough current in the charging system to stop the amp from frying itself, this can be a good way of boosting the bass output of a system. People who compete in Sound Pressure Level (SPL) contests often run their amps into very low impedances to drag as much power as possible from them. In more regular street systems, though, running very low impedances for long periods can overstress amps. So make sure you keep to the impedance recommended by the amp manufacturer.

Decisions, **decisions**

So how do you choose the right amp for your set-up? What should you look for, and almost as important, what should you avoid? How do you know the amp will do what it says on the box, and can you tell if the sales blurb is telling porkies?

For one thing, the tests and features in car audio and car styling mags can give you a good idea. For another, you can make a few assumptions based on the way an amp sounds and is put together. Have a listen to the amp using the same speakers you have or are going to get, and see what you like the best. If you really can't tell the difference, maybe you should just get the one that goes the loudest. You might need the extra volume in a few months' time...

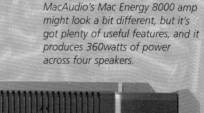

You want bass? The Jonah Lomu special edition amp from Fusion belts out huge amounts of power and is optimised for running a bass-heavy SPL system. How does over 2000watts grab you?

MacAudio's Mac Energy 8000 amp might look a bit different, but it's got plenty of useful features, and it produces 360watts of power across four speakers.

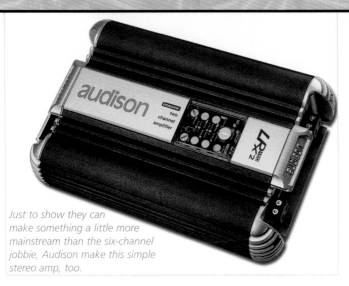

Just to show they can make something a little more mainstream than the six-channel jobbie, Audison make this simple stereo amp, too.

When you get the thing out of the box, you should be able to tell whether it feels full of circuitry or fresh air. There have been amps that look huge on the outside but have very little going on inside – and they could never hope to live up to the over-optimistic '1000watts' stickers plastered across the top panel.

When you handle the amplifier, does it look well made and finished off? If it looks cheaply assembled, it probably is. Are the power and speaker terminals nicely plated and solidly mounted, or are they puny looking, tarnished and going a bit dull already? All these little things should give you an idea of the general quality of the unit and whether or not it will survive in your install.

It is also worth sussing out if the amp appears capable of producing the claimed power output. There's an easy method of checking to see how close it might get – look at the size of the amp's fuse. There's a quick sum that should help you sort the diamonds from the glass.

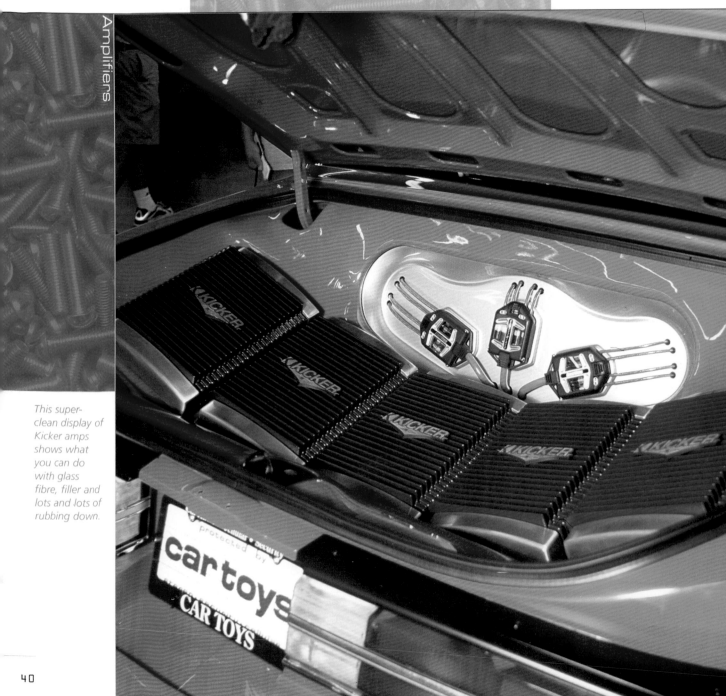

This super-clean display of Kicker amps shows what you can do with glass fibre, filler and lots and lots of rubbing down.

Let's say you find a monster of an amp. It weighs a ton, looks like it'd kill you if it fell on you and has 400watts + 400watts splashed all over its chunky heatsink. It looks like it's just the amp to run your subs, but you want to know if it really can produce 800watts. Well, the sum works out like this.

Almost all amplifiers are about 50 per cent efficient, so to produce 800watts of musical energy it will waste another 800watts as heat. That gives us a 1600watt total. Now if we divide that 1600watt figure by the 12 volts that we have in the vehicle electrical system, we get a figure of 133.33 amperes, which means that our amp will need to chew on 133 amperes of current to produce 800watts of usable power. But when you check the amp's end panel, it's only fitted with a 25 amp fuse. How can that be?

Well, that power figure could be totally meaningless – and it probably is. If it isn't referenced to any particular industry standard in the handbook, who knows under what conditions it can produce this mythical wattage? Maybe it was bolted to an unlimited bench power supply and produced that power output for just a few seconds, before it went pop. Anyway, by working the calculation the other way round, you can see what power output it really has.

If our amplifier can digest 25 amperes of current, and the vehicle voltage is 12 volts, we multiply the two figures together to get 300watts. Not a bad output, but nowhere near the 800 claimed. But when we factor in the 50 per cent efficiency, we have to halve the 300watts to 150watts, which is nowhere near as impressive. And don't laugh – there are plenty of big, impressive (but ultimately cheap) amps like that out there. And they *are* too good to be true.

You are bound to get variations on these figures. Voltage levels in modern cars often get up to around 14 volts, in which case there's much more power for the amp to play with. Also, some amps are more than 50 per cent efficient, so they don't waste as much of their available current. But if you look at the size of the fuse stuck in the side of the unit, you'll get an idea of whether the unit can live up to its billing.

The sums we've just been doing are part of the set of calculations that form Ohm's Law, which is one of the most basic laws of electricity. Once you know your way round it, you can figure out pretty much anything to do with power, resistance, voltage and current. However, the full Ohm's shooting match is too detailed for us to go into here, so consult a good electrical reference book if you want to find out more. For our purposes, it's enough to know whether or not an amp can make its claimed output.

One thing worth bearing in mind: even if a mate has got a loud system with one of these 'too good to be true' amps in it, it doesn't mean it really is doing what it says on the tin. Lots of other factors come into making a system seem loud, so it might be that he or she is getting good results from the 75watts per channel that the amp is actually making. After all, this isn't magic – it's physics. And no one has come up with a way of cheating it yet.

One last thing about amplifiers. Keep them cool. Because they produce heat as well as power for your speakers, you must have some way of getting rid of that heat or the amplifier could get damaged.

Whether you install the amp in an open airspace and allow the heat to rise from the heatsink or put it in a fan-cooled enclosure, please be sure your amp isn't going to fry while it's working hard. And never mount one upside down under a back shelf. That's just asking for trouble.

The sleek-looking Genesis Profile Five is a British designed and made amp that sounds great, looks really cool, and has enough crossover options to run a whole system actively without the need for anything else apart from speakers.

These Stinger linear fans could be just the thing you need to keep your amp rack nice and cool, and stop them overheating as you pound out the tunes.

Speaker's corner

*If you've got a
door this big,
why not fill it
with speakers?
It was made
for it.*

The final pieces in our car stereo jigsaw are the
speakers. These take the electrical signal from the
amplification section and turn it into a
recognisable sound that, hopefully, our ears can
deal with. Speakers come in all different shapes
and sizes and although they are all designed to
do the same basic job, some do it in totally
different ways.

As with the amplifiers, speakers are the
subject of loads of myths, so let's put a few
things straight first of all.

How many times have you heard someone say something like 'I've got 200watt front speakers and 500watt subs', as though this showed just how incredible they are? The power rating on a speaker seems to be the only way of telling someone how good it is, so meaningless figures are thrown about – and those poor souls who don't know any better are taken in by them.

The maximum wattage figure of a speaker has absolutely nothing to do with how good the speaker is going to sound or how loud it will go. It doesn't even have a great deal of meaning when it comes to how much power the speaker can safely deal with, either.

The sound quality of a speaker not only depends on how well it is designed and built, but also on how well it's been installed, and on how good or bad the head unit, processing and amplification are. It's garbage in, garbage out. And if your stonking great speaker is fitted to a flimsy, flappy door panel with two screws instead of six, how well's it going to work?

The better the speakers, the more accurate and faithful they are to the source signal. So stick a £500 pair of component speakers on to a dodgy cassette deck with a puny amp and you'll wonder why those speakers cost £500 at all. But put them into a system that uses top quality gear throughout, and you'll get a good idea why they wilted your credit card.

As for loudness, the sensitivity rating is a little bit more relevant, giving an idea of how much volume the speaker can be expected to produce for the amount of power going into it. But even this is only a very rough guide, and you'll have a better idea of which to choose once you've had a listen to a few in a similar installation and in a similar vehicle to your own.

Just remember, a speaker cannot, will not, and never has produced power on its own. So just because it says 200watts on the box, it doesn't mean there's going to be 200watts flowing through the system. It's a bit like car tyres. Just because the tyres are Z-rated and are safe over 150mph, it doesn't mean the car can do over 150mph.

As for how much power the speaker can really handle, that peak power rating is still a bit dodgy. The RMS rating, or the Continuous power rating, is much more meaningful. Although they are too general to give an absolute indication of how much power a speaker can handle, the continuous rating should enable you to team it up with an amplifier that won't fry it or blow it.

Some manufacturers say they put a peak power figure on their speakers to give you an idea of which of their amps to hook it up to. If they rate an amp at 2x150watts maximum power output, you can stick it up a pair of their 150-watt max speakers without getting terminal meltdown of the voice coils.

While that will definitely help, closer inspection will probably reveal that you've put 50-watt continuous speakers on to a 50-watt-per-channel amplifier. Not quite as impressive as the 300-watt set-up you thought you'd bought, but not likely to blow itself up either.

You should also remember that you can often do more damage with a small amp on a big speaker than the other way round. It is very unusual to come across speakers that have been blown up by using an amp that's too big for them to handle.

But it's far more common to see ones that have been burned out because a head unit or small external booster was turned up so far that it sent loads of distortion into the speaker and fried the voice coil instead of blowing it apart. It would seem that an under-worked 200-watt amp will feed a nice clean signal into a 50-watt speaker all day long. But a 150-watt speaker could easily get fried by all the distortion of a 20-watt amp when it's really cranked.

Having cleared up that little myth, the next step is to look at the different types of speakers, what they do, and how to get good results from them.

Big speaker, little speaker

We've already touched on octaves and frequency bands in chapter three, but we need a bit more detail here.

Audible sound is generally thought of as covering the range from 20Hz to 20,000Hz – or 20 kiloHertz – and is split up into ten octaves. The range of an octave just refers to double or half of another frequency,

Alpine's three-way SPS-6939S is one of their versions of the popular 6x9 speaker size.

so one octave higher than 150Hz is 300Hz, and one octave lower than 5000Hz is 2500Hz. So if you start doing the octave maths at 20Hz, it more or less works out that 20,000Hz is ten octaves higher. That is: 20-40Hz, 40-80Hz, 80-160Hz, 160-320Hz, 320-640Hz, 640-1280Hz, and so on.

These ten octaves are further split up into the four ranges of sub bass, mid bass, mid range and treble. Although there are slight variations, these areas are split roughly like this – sub bass is 20-100Hz, mid bass is 100-400Hz, mid range is 400-5000Hz, and treble is 5000Hz and up. These are rough guidelines to the frequency splits, and in many cases, speakers can work beyond these points.

Before we get in to the more upmarket speaker ranges, let's have a quick look at the rest of the field. A quick glance at a demonstration stand in a car audio shop shows that speakers take all sizes and shapes, but there's a lot more to them than that. The

Without a rear seat-back, the possibilities for fitting sub woofers just get easier.

Speaker's corner

The Alpine SWR-1540 sub not only looks the part, it can crank out the bass, too. It can handle a continuous 500watts, or a peak of 1500watts, so it should last the distance in any system.

For an easy bass fix, this Jensen tube can be fitted with a couple of fabric straps, wired up to an amp, and away you go.

main difference is that some speakers are supposed to be used as full-range, jack-of-all-trades, while others are designed to handle specific frequency bands and work with other units to give the complete audio picture window.

The quality and price of full-range speakers varies widely, starting at the very basic single-cone things that, years ago, used to be found hooked up to push button radios in cars. These were never expected to sound brilliant, and they didn't. Sizes were limited, too.

Next up are dual-cone speakers, which have a small sub-cone fitted in the centre of the main cone. This is supposed to respond to the treble content of the signal, giving a better top-end response and a clearer sound.

Above that is the coaxial, or two-way, which uses a separate small drive unit for high frequencies and the main cone for everything else. By adding a proper tweeter with its own passive crossover to play the high notes, these speakers often performed better than the dual-cones.

One step further up the ladder are the triaxial, or three-way, speakers. With most, the two smaller drivers seem to be designed to handle the high frequencies, rather than the mids and highs. That's to be expected, though, because the largest cone will only really sort out the mid bass/mid range area and won't dip down into the low-bass region. There are even a few four-way speakers that have three tweeters in them, but they aren't that wonderful to listen to – unless you're a bat.

As well as the differences in drive unit configuration, these full-range speakers also come in different shapes and sizes. Apart from the most common round speakers, you can get oval ones, too. As far as sizes go, full-range stuff goes from about 87mm right up to 200mm, and the 6x9in speaker is very popular.

The widest choice of different models occurs in the 100mm, 130mm and 160/165mm areas, which also happen to be the most common original equipment (OE) sizes. There are a few exceptions in the OE market, such as the 100x150mm or 125x175mm oval drivers, but most vehicle manufacturers have stayed with round speakers.

While there are some very good integrated speakers on the market, the best quality comes from a system that uses

If you ever see a speaker like this, you've seriously damaged it. Actually, it's just a diagram to let you see what goes into a JL Audio sub woofer.

individual drive units for specific parts of the frequency range. By fitting component drivers instead of integrated ones, you move up on to a whole new level of performance.

Depth **gauges**

The sub woofer, as the name implies, provides the real grunt behind the music that comes from the very low bass. Most subs will be playing 100Hz or lower, depending on system and tuning, and in some applications they'll be felt rather than heard. However they're going to be used, there are a few rules for getting the best performance from your subs.

For size, subs go from 100mm – yes, that's four inches – to more than 30in. In fact, a couple of much larger speakers have been built, but they were made specifically for competition use and were never designed to go into production. And let's face it – who is going to find room for a five-foot speaker that needs thousands of watts to get it moving?

This Magnat Aggressor 6000 sub is a monstrous 63cm across. Yes, that's over two feet in old money. Big enough for ya?

The multiple installation capabilities of these Alpine SXE-1750 mids let them fit into lots of vehicles equipped with 16cm DIN speaker apertures. And they'll sound loads better than anything fitted by a motor manufacturer.

These SXE-0825 speakers don't look it, but they are only 3.5in across. Better than the original stuff they'd be replacing, but where's the bass coming from?

Like everything else in car audio, sub woofer designers are always trying new ideas to get better performance, or to get decent performance for a lower price. As well as trying new cone materials and suspension designs, manufacturers are even playing with the shape of the speaker itself. At the time of writing, you could not only find round subs, but you could also go for hexagonal, square or triangular woofers if you wanted. Whether or not any of these is truly a leap forward in sound quality is yet to be proved, but they do allow you to leave very little wasted space when filling a wall with woofers.

Sub designers are always trying to make the woofer work in a really small box, too, so it doesn't take over all of your luggage space like early sub designs used to. These days, it's easy to find a speaker that will fit into a box of less than one cubic foot, but that still drops like a brick and hits like a truck. So unless you have a tiny boot, there will be a sub available to do the job you want, in the space you have.

If you really can't spare any luggage space for a bit of thump, there's always the infinite baffle (often incorrectly called the free-air) woofer. Infinite baffle basically means the speaker is totally separated from the listening environment, but isn't actually enclosed in a cabinet of its own. While this sounds like a contradiction, it just means that the speaker is fitted to a baffle between the cabin and the outside, or more usually the boot.

As a result, you can stick a couple of subs on your back shelf and let them thump away in the boot while you get the bass benefit in the car. It sounds like a great idea and can work really well in a lot of cars, but it isn't a quick job to get the speakers

If you want a sub woofer that looks like it could do serious damage, they don't look a lot meaner than the Destructor 1200 from Magnat.

This cutaway shot shows how different the Aliante sub woofer is from more conventional designs.

performing to the best of their ability.

A lot of work has to be done to strengthen the back shelf and the boot has to be as sealed from the cabin as possible. Any air leaks between the interior and the boot will spoil the bass performance. And you need to run speakers that are designed specially for the job otherwise the bass will be dire and the speaker could easily be damaged.

Boxing clever

Apart from the infinite baffle sub, which can happily live on a back shelf, all other woofers need some form of enclosure to make them work in a reasonable manner and to stop them jumping apart.

When you buy a woofer, it should come with a recommended box size and type. If you're buying it from a specialist dealer, he or she can probably recommend a box design and size that will let it perform to the best of its ability. But what are the options and what makes one better than another?

The simplest and probably most popular sub enclosure is the sealed box, which is also known as an air suspension, acoustic suspension or second order enclosure. For most car audio enthusiasts, it's the best one to have a go at constructing. Once you've worked out how big to build it, cut the pieces accurately, and glued and screwed them together solidly, the woofer and enclosure's performance should be as described by the manufacturer.

In a sealed box, the woofer's behaviour is tightly controlled by the trapped air inside the enclosure. The more the speaker cone moves out from, and back into, the box, the more the air inside tries to oppose the force. The main advantages of this design are the lack of distortion and high power-handling at low frequencies, as well as the overall smoothness and sound quality when the box design is spot on.

The next most popular design is the ported box, also known as the vented or bass-reflex enclosure. This box differs from the sealed enclosure because it has some form of vent or pipe that allows the energy inside the box to augment the output from the driver, so giving more bass output. This gives the immediate advantage that a woofer in a ported enclosure produces 3dB more than if it was in a sealed box.

Unfortunately, a vented enclosure isn't as straightforward to build as a sealed box. The real variable comes from the box tuning, which needs to be optimised correctly. If not, the woofer's performance will be lacking and it could damage itself. The three factors in the vented enclosure's design – namely, the air volume in the box, the resonant effect of the port and the speaker's parameters – all need to be matched closely to get the best results.

Most speaker manufacturers recommend an enclosure design and often give all the dimensions you need to build the best box for the woofer you want to buy. If they don't give you that kind of information, you could always try getting it from the person who's trying to sell it to you. If he or she can't help, maybe you should be looking at a different woofer – or a different supplier.

Beyond the sealed and vented enclosures, you start getting into more esoteric designs using several chambers, multiple ports and things like Isobaric woofer mounting. These more complicated enclosures are even more susceptible to poor performance brought on through miscalculation and incorrect construction, so in this book we'll just mention them and move on.

While the sealed and vented boxes might not be the absolute best at doing everything, they are the best all-rounders and are the easiest to build correctly. All you have to do is to

This shows a typical three-way integrated speaker, with its two small high-frequency drivers sitting on a centre mount surrounded by the bass cone.

This Fusion ready-made sub box lets you see both sides of the subs as they drop the bass-line. That's if you can focus your wobbling eyes...

Speaker's corner

remember a couple of things before you go chopping the wood for your enclosure.

Use good quality materials, measure everything twice before you cut it and get the joints properly glued and screwed to prevent leaks. You'll find more info on box building in Chapter 12.

But if you don't fancy building your own sub enclosure, there are still a few ways to get that all-important thump. Most manufacturers sell ready-boxed subs that just need bolting into your motor, and if a big square enclosure is too much, there are bass tubes as well.

Tubes are simply round sub enclosures and they're available in ported or sealed designs in many different sizes. Some people regard them as a downmarket idea that never really caught on, but lots of cars have been fitted with bass tubes and their owners love them. They combine decent bass performance with easy fitting and the small ones take up very little room indeed.

Stick a couple of these Jonah Lomu subs onto a Jonah amplifier and you can do some serious damage to your car's integrity. These look bombproof and they are only the ten-inchers.

48

A simple 6x9 two-way shows exactly what's meant by a coaxial speaker. Two separate drivers sharing the same axis.

Get your kicks

Mid-bass drivers are probably the most overlooked in car audio. But as well as providing a great sonic benefit, they can also bring their own problems.

To get dedicated mid basses into a system, it really means running a four-way speaker set-up, and that can cause difficulty with crossovers and phasing. It can also be very expensive to run enough amplification and electronics to get the whole system to work as well as it should.

In almost all cases correct installation and tuning of decent mid range drivers and sub woofers can put the mid-bass kick into a system, without adding the complication of extra speakers.

Middle of the range

Mid-range drivers have a very difficult job to do, mainly because the range of sounds they handle is the most important. Most of the fundamental tones of the human voice and a lot of musical instruments happen in this area, so if the speaker doesn't do a good job replaying them accurately, your tunes will never sound right.

Unlike the wide range of sub sizes, mids generally run between 100mm and 165mm, with a couple of 200mm exceptions. Cone profiles and materials vary considerably, though, with everything from treated paper to aluminium used in the search for the perfect combination. At least everyone seems to have settled on the shape as being round, for very good technical reasons.

Unlike a sub woofer, almost all mid-range speakers don't need to be fitted in a cabinet of any particular volume, but they do need a solid base and to have their rear wave isolated from the listening area. As you'll see in the chapter on speaker installation, a door speaker can have its performance substantially improved by a decent mounting and some proper sound deadening.

Treble top

The tweeters are generally the smallest speakers in the system. They handle the high frequencies and need careful integration to ensure they blend in with the mids. When they do, you hear your music as a seamless sound. When they don't, you can tell that some bits come from the tweets and others come from the mid ranges.

Apart from providing the sparkly, tinkly bits of the music, tweeters play a very important role in giving us some cues about the space that the original recording was made in. And they have to do both these jobs without sounding harsh.

Tweeters are subject to just as much experimentation as mid-ranges and they come in different sizes, materials and mounting designs. While you should choose the speaker set – mids and tweeters – that sounds best to you, you also have to think about what's actually going to fit in your car.

This is where a decent dealer comes in handy again, because they'll let you listen to various sets of speakers that will sound good *and* do it in your car. You can always make completely new mountings for a component set that won't go in your motor's original locations, but be led by the sound quality first. You can always think about getting into making door builds or kick panel enclosures if the sound you prefer the most comes from speakers that need the extra work.

You don't have to build a sub box from wood, you can always go mad and make it from 25mm-thick perspex. If you do that though, don't forget the neon.

A regular two-way passive crossover, this time from Fusion, hence the green lid.

very wide and the vocalists and musicians were placed exactly where they should be.

Secondly, by having a lower crossover point than a conventional tweeter, the phase problems created by a crossover were moved out of the area that the ear was very sensitive to. The better the compression driver, the lower the crossover point. In a couple of pairs, that crossover point was about 400Hz, where a conventional mid-range would be handing over to a mid-bass driver. By having one speaker cover such a wide range, the final sound promised to be spectacular.

The only problems with horn drivers were their weird letterbox shape and, with the really top-notch ones, their cost. Because they required a more involved installation – and because of that nasty little money problem – horn drivers seem to have just about disappeared from use.

What's NXT?

A new speaker technology is just beginning to emerge in car audio. It's the flat panel driver, developed by a company called NXT.

This new driver type is said to have plenty of benefits for in-car use, mainly because it doesn't require an enclosure. It doesn't operate like a conventional point-source driver, so it can also be integrated into most flat areas, such as dashboards, door panels, headlinings and parcel shelves.

Although NXT appears to be working with various motor manufacturers, at the time of writing no car has been released with a production version of the flat driver system. So we'll have to wait and see how it performs once it's offered in place of normal speakers. If it lives up to the claims, it could be a very interesting piece of kit.

One of Panasonic's entries in the powered sub-box market, this unit only uses a 12cm bass driver, and is small enough to fit under some car seats.

Round the horn

The horn, or compression driver, is a speaker that has been around for a few years, mainly in competition installations. These weird-looking things are actually mid/high-frequency drivers that have a very wide frequency response and they were designed to do a couple of jobs.

Firstly, they were shaped to disperse their output across a vehicle in such a way that the listeners got no impression of speakers being fitted at each side of the car. Instead, the stage sounded

If you want wacky-looking sub designs, how's this Pioneer TS-W1201 for you?

06

Did you see that?

This Blaupunkt TravelPilot widescreen monitor lets you see all your route details as you're travelling and being prompted to make turns by the unit's voice.

These wireless headphones from Alpine are designed for back-seat passengers who are watching one programme while the driver listens to something else in the front of the car.

A four-speaker eight-track system used to make jaws drop a few years ago. But recent technical advances mean that it now takes something a bit more elaborate to wow a crowd. And we know exactly what you need.

A kicking system really needs some form of TV, and something cool to show on it. That means you can hook up a video or DVD player to show movies, or you can add a games console and twiddle your controller, accompanied by a sound system that will blow your home TV into the weeds.

Did you see that?

Alpine's DVA-5205P one-box in-dash DVD player gives superb picture quality and a digital output that contains the necessary soundtrack info to surround you in the movie.

This Alpine NVE-N077PS DVD GPS navigation system can guide you all around Europe on the information contained on one DVD, and can talk to you in one of eight languages. You'll never get lost again. Anywhere...

Okay, a head unit with a built-in screen isn't going to be cheap, but once you've bought it, it's going to last a good few years. And you can always take it from car to car. If the screen is part of the head unit, you won't need to have lots of extra installation done to get it fitted. Well, that's always provided your car has a reasonable head unit position from standard. If it isn't, you'll just have to sell the car and buy one with a more sensible radio slot. Only kidding.

A mobile cinema installation can be a big expense, though, so you should think seriously about what you want to install and why you want it. If you travel with a few small passengers who constantly ask 'are we there yet?' you could probably get away with a simple single-screen video system that constantly showed Barney cartoons.

As the kids get older and want more sophistication from their in-car entertainment, you'll be able to take advantage of the fact that prices will have fallen further. You'll then be able to add a games console or more screens to give them some choice over their viewing.

But if you want the system to be a bit of a showpiece when you go cruising with your mates, you're going to have to go for something a bit more wild than a single screen and a video player. Whatever you buy to produce the pictures, it needs to be hooked into an impressive audio system or the magic will be lost. Where and how many screens you fit into your car then depends on the budget you can scrape together.

If you don't fancy a head unit with a screen built into it, you've still got a few other TV options. The cheapest is a small CRT television, which uses a tiny version of a normal haunted fishtank and can be bought quite cheaply. It's a bit more involved to install because it will be a small cube-shaped box rather than a flat panel like an LCD screen, but if you want to drop the TV into a centre console, you should stand half a chance of it going in without too much effort.

One big advantage of a tubed television – apart from its relative lack of cost – is that the viewing angle can be much wider than a flat-panel TV. Fix one in your centre console and almost anyone in the car should get a good picture without needing to stick their head between the front seats. But they aren't without their drawbacks.

The main one has to be their standard non-widescreen format.

This is the wireless transmitter that runs two pairs of the headphones across the page. It can even send different signals to each pair if the wearers are watching different TV programmes.

If you've got a decent video or DVD player providing the picture, you'll struggle when you play a big budget movie. You'll miss out on half the action because the picture will be letterboxed and therefore very small.

As for flat LCD-type screens, there are lots to choose from and they come in various sizes and styles. You fit them in the dash, the centre console, the rear headrests and even have them drop down from a housing screwed to the roof. It just depends on who's going to be watching the picture, and when.

There are plenty of widescreen monitors available now, too, as well as lots of regular-shape ones. So you need to choose what you need based on what you're going to be playing on it, and where you'll be fitting it in your car.

Location is also a consideration with games consoles. You have to decide who is going to play the games, where they are going to sit to play them and where they expect to watch the screen. If

This is a drop-down monitor that's usually fitted in the car's roof for the rear-seat passengers.

This Alpine monitor can fit into smaller headrests or dash apertures to show navigation info or films, depending on who's watching, and who's driving.

fav-2000 7" WIDE SCREEN MULTIMEDIA

VOL + · PRESET ▼ · PRESET ▲ · ◀ TUNE · T

VOL · VIDEO · MEMO

To get the full widescreen effect, you need a widescreen monitor. This is Alpine's TME-M750 which we have a go at fitting in Chapter 10.

you answer 'in the front' or 'while I'm driving' to any of those, think again. Plod really doesn't like that sort of thing going on.

More and more cars are having games consoles fitted, and the Sony PS2 has the added bonus of a DVD player built in. With the installation, the biggest question seems to be how to get the 240-volt unit playing in a car. Luckily for some systems, 12-volt boards are available to replace the mains converter, which means the unit becomes a dedicated in-car unit.

But for those who don't want to lose the option of taking it back into the house to play with, there are various 12- to 240-volt adapters that convert the car's voltage up to the required amount, so the console can be plugged straight in like it is indoors.

Any night is **movie** night

If you want to play films in your mobile cinema, you have two main options. You can either choose to play your video collection on a large cumbersome video player that doesn't give you instant track access or real surround sound, or you can go for a neat, dash-mounted DVD player that gives you all that, and more.

Well, it isn't actually as clear-cut as that and video playback in a car does have a lot going for it. Tapes are cheaper than DVDs and the players are generally far less expensive than their DVD alternative, even if they do take up a bit more room.

You can even buy plug-in systems that have a video player in a bag that straps on to a seatback, and a screen mounted on a removable arm. They're a great idea for keeping kids quiet on a long journey, but the street cred is a bit lacking. What you need is a built-in bit of kit that looks the part and does the business.

Fitting a video into a dash can be a major job that requires a fair bit of rebuilding, simply because of their size. We've seen it done, but it seems to be on cars that had gloveboxes the size of a suitcase to start with. Even then, they had no space left after the installation.

On balance, videos are probably something to be fitted in the boot. If you think that makes operating them a bit of a pain, don't worry. Almost all dedicated in-car videos come with a remote control, and a receiver eye that can be fitted in the cabin. This can be fitted on the dash or in an air vent. Then all you do is point the remote roughly at the front of the car and things happen on screen. It looks really cool.

Even cooler, though, is DVD, which seems to be the biggest thing in A/V at the moment. The shiny silver discs look just like CDs but they store far more information. And when they contain a film with a mental surround-soundtrack that's full of effects, they make stereo videos seem tame.

Your audio system has to be able to replay this information correctly or the film might fall a bit flat, particularly if it's a real blockbuster. But when you look at the superior picture and sound quality of DVDs, they're worth the extra, even if you have to wait a while before you can afford to get the full benefit.

Unlike video players, some DVD units are DIN-sized so they can be fitted straight into a dash opening without any trouble at all. This means easy disc swapping on the go and fewer boxes of electronics taking up

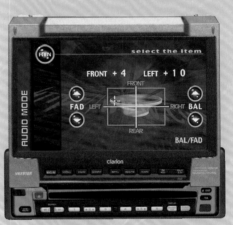

Blaupunkt's TravelPilot dispenses with the need for a separate screen by showing all the necessary navigation prompts on its built-in display.

Clarion's VRX918R is not only a pop-out widescreen monitor unit, it has a touch-screen so you only have to tap the function you want on the display, and it happens.

luggage room. But it's also another unit fitted where a tea-leaf might take a shine to it.

As well as single-disc in-dash units, there are a couple of DVD autochangers, which work just like a regular CD 'changer, so you can choose from several films, all loaded up and ready to go.

Clarion's answer to in-car DVD is the DVS970Z. It has a DIN-sized player that can be fitted anywhere in the car, but a separate display for mounting in the cabin. It comes with this multi-function remote that allows full control without the need to stretch to the display.

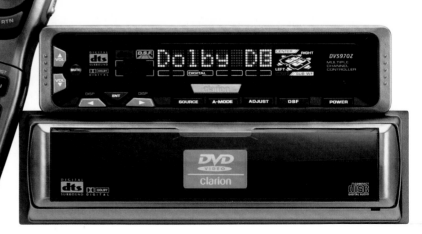

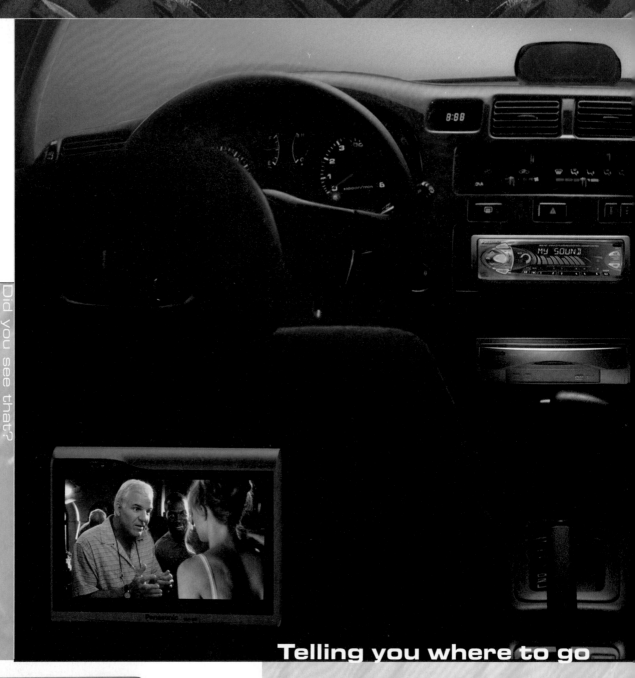

Did you see that?

Telling you where to go

Once the screen's fitted into your motor, you can always add something that'll be really useful when you're driving – a navigation system. True, there are a couple of one-box systems around that don't need a proper screen to show you turns and street names and stuff. But a navi unit hooked into a screen will give you decent maps and a better idea of where you should be heading when you approach a weird junction.

If you do go for a navigation system, you have to thank the Pentagon for allowing the Global Positioning Satellite information to be accurate enough so that the little box of tricks fitted in your car can tell where you are to within a few feet.

The newest systems keep all their information on a DVD, which

This is a complete Pioneer DVD navigation system, showing the DVD player, separate screen and complicated remote control. This will operate all the unit's functions, so a couple of hours with the manual would be a good idea.

means they can carry stacks of information about whole continents, and you can access that info in a matter of seconds. If you're running out of fuel, for instance, the system can show you the nearest filling stations. Low on grub, it'll point out eateries, too. A DVD navi can even show you points of interest if into sightseeing. Their only potential problem is the initial cost. And that, like all things electronic, will fall as chips get cheaper and more people buy them.

Hard drives in your car

The integrated in-car computer hasn't really started to take off yet, but systems are either under development or already out there. One of the first stand-alone units was QPC, but it only made a bit of a splash in the US before being moved from cars to the massive RV, or recreational vehicle, market.

QPC had a bombproof hard-drive system developed for use in military Humvees and could be interfaced with a remote control

keyboard and a screen to give all manner of cool functions. Unfortunately, it didn't take off as well as they'd hoped in the in-car field, hence the shift into RVs, where a whole family could compute on the move.

A couple of years ago, Clarion launched a system called Auto PC, which used a head unit that ran Windows CE as the operating platform. Again, big things were expected and even Bill Gates turned up at the official launch, but it seems that the aftermarket wasn't really ready to redesign the way it installed car audio systems to allow a computer to do the work.

It looks as though computer integration will really hit it big when the vehicle manufacturers give us a dash screen and a mouse on the steering wheel. Then we've just got to hope that drivers will be able to concentrate on driving the car *and* driving the computer. It could be messy.

New tech and Old Bill

As we went to press, the legal side of TV screens in cars is a bit of a grey area. It all boils down to what you are playing – or have the ability to play – on the screen, who can see it, and what kind of screen you have.

Most of the law is written around having a cathode ray tube (CRT) device in the vehicle. Since most mobile TVs are based around flat screens, that's the first grey area. Then the copper would have to prove that the screen was being used to display something other than vehicle status, location, or destination information.

Basically, that means he's got to prove that you were driving, or someone else was driving, while the screen was showing something other than vehicle or navigation information. Even audio functions could conceivably be called vehicle status info.

Having said all that, please make sure you don't do anything daft like try to watch the latest episode of *Coronation Street* or catch up on a movie while you're driving. It's way too distracting. So use your head, and watch your TV only when you're parked up.

When you get close to a turn, most navigation systems will show you exactly where you are going through the junction, as well as telling you where to go.

If you have the space to fit one, a widescreen monitor like this Pioneer AVD-W8000 really helps when playing games or movies.

Basic installation techniques

Before you start tearing into your new car stereo install, there are some techniques you should be aware of and a few tools that are worth having. If you're sticking to really basic stuff, you can probably get away with a couple of screwdrivers and some wire cutters, but once you start getting more involved, your toolkit will have to get bigger.

It's a lot easier to get decent equipment at a sensible price these days, and availability of quite specialised stuff is very good. You can equip a workshop with some really neat gear just by calling one of the specialist mail-order tool and fastener suppliers who advertise on TV.

Unless you're thinking of starting up in the installation business, you don't need to go mad and build a separate wood room and trimming shop on the side of your house. Just about everything in this book was carried out in a medium-sized garage.

Many of the hand tools you'll need are pretty general, but some makes of car need special kinds of screwdrivers or sockets to undo and replace most of their parts. The best way to find out what you need is to consult a workshop manual, which Haynes publishes for almost every car on the road.

The right manual for your car will also show you how the whole thing comes apart. You might think you've got a pretty good idea how to get your door panel off, for instance, but you could easily

Stinger noise deadening mats come in many types for different applications.

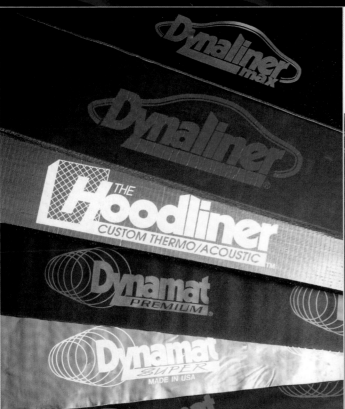

Dynamat offer plenty of different types of mat to go in different areas of the car bodywork.

If you just want to do the doors of your car, a kit like this Dynamat Xtreme pack could be just what you need.

miss a hidden fastener. You'll only know about this when you do some very expensive damage as you wrench the panel off the door, leaving half of it behind.

All **tooled** up

Most simple toolkits will have a reasonable cross-section of spanners, sockets, screwdrivers and pliers to tackle straightforward car maintenance. These are ideal for stereo installation. Because we aren't going too deeply into the mechanical stuff, you won't need the really heavy-duty gear.

A lot of car accessory stores sell toolkits that are quite comprehensive and reasonable quality, and they don't bust your wallet either. Avoid cheap spanners that stretch open and ruin the bolt head, though, and nasty sockets that split open the first time you put any force through them.

Apart from the specialised kit that your vehicle might demand, such as Torx drivers or Allen keys, you're going to need tools for messing around with wire. A pair of good wire cutters is an absolute necessity and some decent crimping pliers won't go amiss either.

With these two items in your toolkit, you'll be able to cut cables to the correct length for the job, and then stick a terminal on the end that won't pull off at the first sign of strain. If you get deeply into fitting gear, you can get different sizes of cutters

If you start installing car audio, you'll need some decent screwdrivers, and you'll need a few sizes, too.

Look carefully at the tips and you can just see the difference between the Phillips on the left and the Pozidrives on the right.

A good socket set will help you whip your car apart in moments. Just be sure you don't break anything, or forget where anything goes.

Wire cutters will be on the shopping list, too. Get some medium-size ones at first, and then you can buy more specialised ones as you get more involved with installation.

and more weird and wonderful terminal pliers. To start with, though, just go for the popular ones.

Screwdrivers come in many different sizes and types, and although some of them look almost exactly the same, they aren't really interchangeable. I looked in a Snap-On tools catalogue and found that they produce screwdrivers to service 12 different styles of screwhead. What's really amazing is that this number doesn't account for the numerous sizes and lengths of screwdriver available for each of the 12 designs. Screwdrivers took up 18 pages in the catalogue.

The most common mistake is to swap Phillips and Pozidrive screwdrivers and fasteners without realising there's much difference. In a lot of cases, they are almost the same, but when you start using the wrong 'driver on factory-tightened fasteners or on the end of an electric screwdriver, you'll wreck the screwhead before you know it.

This is of particular note to Ford owners, because Ford always

These are all crimping pliers that handle different types of terminals. The yellow-handled ones at the top right are probably the sort you'll start with, but you might need a couple of the others as you become more involved.

used Pozidrive fasteners up until they diversified into Torx and Hex heads, so if you have something that looks like a factory-fitted crosshead fastener on your Ford, make sure you attack it with a Pozidrive screwdriver.

There's another good reason for getting the manual and reading it thoroughly. It allows you to pick up an idea of what normal tools are needed to get into the various nooks and crannies of your vehicle before you start a job. That way, you don't start taking something apart and disable the car, only to find you've got to put it all back together to drive to the nearest supplier for the tool you're missing.

If you are going to start hunting around for wiring in your car, you really should get a multimeter. With so much computer equipment fitted to modern cars, you shouldn't use a test light to try to find which wires are live and which aren't. You could do a delicate microchip an expensive nasty if you accidentally short it

Although they look pretty similar, you can see the extra points on the Pozidrive screw that let the screwdriver bite harder into the fastener. The Phillips screw is the plain four-pointed one below the Pozidrive.

These are automatic wire strippers which do a great job of stripping the insulator from wire before it's soldered or terminated.

out or connect it to a live feed when you didn't intend to.

A multimeter will stop you damaging the vehicle systems while you play 'find the feed' and you can use it for checking other things, such as speaker condition, speaker system impedances and finding a good system earth point. Like the other tools we've mentioned, multimeters are now inexpensive and widely available.

A soldering iron is also vital. These are available in so many different sizes and types, but for most of the ICE installer's needs, a good gas-powered one is just the job.

Being powered by lighter gas has several advantages, as well as a few disadvantages. The obvious benefits are that there are no wires trailing around the car when you're working and you can do jobs when there isn't any mains power handy. Very useful if you're doing a quick repair halfway down your drive.

The biggest drawbacks are that some gas irons don't get up to a fantastic temperature, so thick wires take ages to solder – or they don't join properly at all. Either that or the thing runs out of

A decent multimeter can save you a lot of money as well as helping you do the job better.

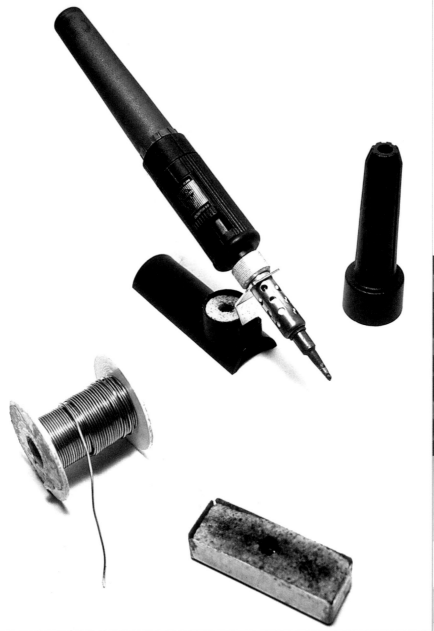

A good gas-powered soldering iron like this one gives plenty of heat for bigger soldering jobs, but it's also small enough for fiddly jobs.

Mixing polyester resin is best done in these plastic pots. When the resin sets, you can flex the pot sides and the resin cracks out, leaving the pot clean to start again.

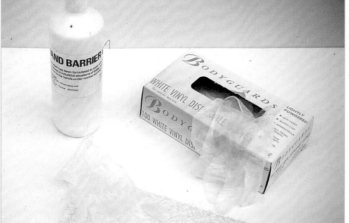

Hand and skin protection is vital when working with glass fibre. Use barrier cream and gloves.

gas in the middle of a job. This only happens a couple of times before you make sure you've refilled the gas cylinder *before* you start using it on the new joint.

If you get really into car audio installing, you'll probably start working with glass fibre and resin, but you don't need many tools for this. Once you've got some accurate measuring scales for sorting out mixing batch sizes and catalyst amounts, you only need some strong scissors for the matting and a roller to force out air bubbles from the laminations. Protective gloves and long sleeved clothing are also a must.

The other important item for your workshop is some form of workbench. The most popular Workmate-style benches are great for almost all eventualities, but you can get away with a couple of beer crates if you're really stuck. The good thing is that the majority of large DIY stores have incredibly cheap alternatives to the well-known branded stuff.

A good fibre roller, sharp scissors and throwaway paint brushes are needed to cut and resin the glass fibre matting.

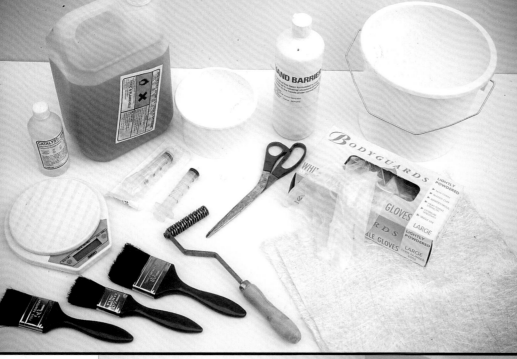

Here's the full glass fibre kit that you'll need. Try to find your local glass fibre supplier in Yellow Pages and you'll save a fortune over buying the stuff from motor accessory shops. Buying chopped-strand mat in bulk also means it's less wasteful.

You have to be spot on when measuring hardener into resin, so accurate scales or syringes should be used to get the required mixture.

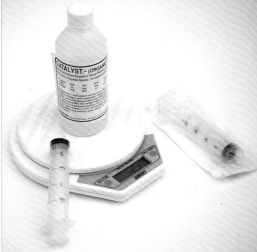

Power play

Apart from mechanical tools, a more involved ICE install may require a few woodworking and power tools to take care of the chopping and shaping of custom fabrications. Again, you don't need that many to get going, and with the increased number of monster DIY stores, a good selection of inexpensive power tools is readily available. Okay, so a cheap jigsaw might last only a couple of minutes on a building site, but if you're just cutting MDF sheets for making sub boxes every now and then, it'll probably do fine.

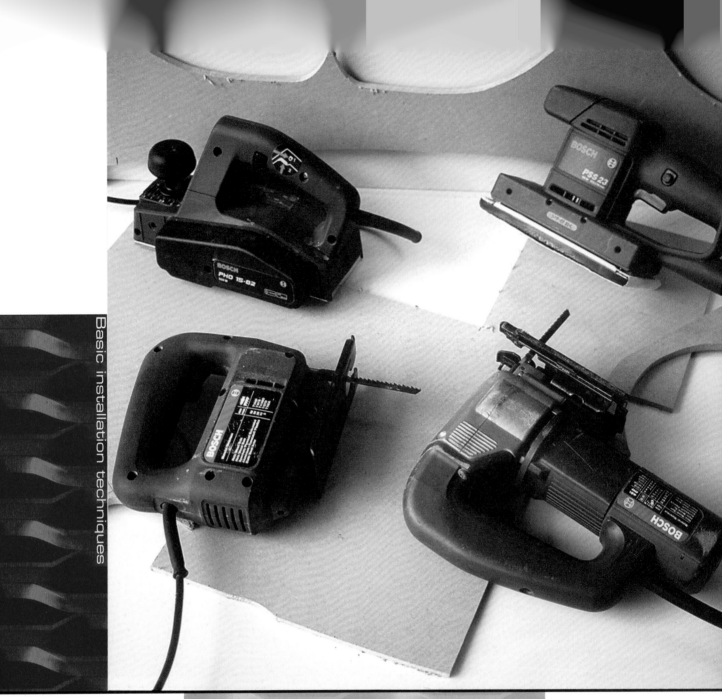

>

The most important thing is the sharpness of the blade you use. If you have a weak jigsaw and a very sharp blade, you won't be running the jiggie long enough for it to overheat. But run it with a blunt blade – one that's wearing through the wood rather than slicing it – and you could easily burn out the motor.

Although the budget gear probably isn't as good as the semi-pro stuff, you've got to think of how much you're going to use it. We've seen drill, jigsaw and sander sets that have been on sale for less than the cost of an hour's labour at a garage, so you can get kitted out for not a lot.

Be **careful** out there

With power tools and workshop goodies, safety techniques and equipment are vital. Sure, it's probably really boring, but ending up in hospital

With a few power tools you can cut, shape, and sand your in-car projects quickly and easily, and the tools don't have to cost the earth these days.

being stitched back together is far worse, so it's worth giving it a little thought. Anything that's harder than you – screwdrivers, pliers, cutters, you name it – can make a painful hole in you if it has enough force behind it when it slips.

The hands of most professional installers have small pale reminders of times when something proved sharp enough to pierce their skin, even when they thought it couldn't. So please be careful when doing anything on your car that involves any amount of force, or anything that might be sharp.

The chances for blood-soaked mayhem become even greater with power tools. Jigsaws can get through flesh and bone remarkably quickly, as can electric drills. If you're cutting something with a jigsaw, do it so the blade is moving away from you. Make sure the thing you are cutting is adequately supported, and check underneath that you aren't going to run into anything electrical, valuable, useful or fleshy.

If, for instance, you're drilling a hole in a small piece of wood, do it on a bench, not on your knee. And get used to releasing the pressure on the drill before it has broken through the other side of what you're drilling. That way, if you do hit something you shouldn't, there's less weight behind the drill pushing it in.

It's also worth considering protecting your eyes and ears. Eye protection is vital if you're drilling and cutting anything that can make splinters or shards. After all, you can't drive your car if you can't see, right? And hearing protection is a good idea if you're using noisy power tools in a confined space for a long time. What's the point of a decent stereo if you can't hear half of it for the ringing in your ears?

The final thing to protect is your breathing. This applies when you are chopping or sanding MDF, or using something with noxious fumes like glass fibre resin. MDF is made from fibres of wood bonded together in a particularly nasty gloop.

The dust that comes off MDF as it is cut or sanded is incredibly fine and the particles can play havoc with your lungs. At the very least, use a small dust mask to stop it going up your nose and down your throat. It gives you a fighting chance of not sneezing brown goo for days after you've finished the job.

When working with glass fibre, a dust mask is going to be a lot less use in preventing you from breathing in the resin fumes, but it still keeps the minute glass fibres from irritating your lungs. It's best to work where there's a good through-flow of fresh air to get rid of the fumes so that you don't end up high as a kite while building your kick panel enclosures.

You also need to cover up as much of your skin as possible when using glass fibre. Glass fibres are an horrendous irritant and they have a nasty habit of not being very noticeable when you're actually doing the job. But as soon as you finish and try to wash them off, you'll be itching for hours. When you're doing anything with glass fibre, it's a good idea to get disposable rubber gloves and wear something with long sleeves so that you can minimise your exposure to the fibres and the dust.

A basic jigsaw with a sharp blade will chop any amount of MDF or plywood for you.

A third-sheet orbital sander makes easy work of rubbing down heavy filler and MDF. Just make sure you don't breathe the dust.

A more sophisticated variable-speed jigsaw would only be a worthwhile purchase if you went into installing car audio for a living.

A few ideas

In answer to the 'what kind of system should I buy?' question, we are most likely to advise something that uses a good head unit, dedicated amplification, decent front speakers and some form of separate sub bass reproduction. If all you want to do is listen to music – rather than go all-out on a full in-car cinema system – we aren't going to recommend shoehorning 24 speakers, 12 amps and three different source units into your vehicle. Remember the KISS principle – Keep It Simple, Stupid – and you won't go far wrong.

Some **techniques to try**

If that sounds dull, think about why you want to fit a car stereo system in the first place. If it's only because all your mates have got them, and you aren't actually that fussed about music, maybe you should find another hobby to throw cash at. If you really love music but also want to have a big system to impress your mates, you can still do it if you KISS the install and the equipment. Fit good gear properly and everyone who hears it will be blown away. Trust us.

A decent system can be made up of a head unit, separate front and sub amplification – even if it's part of the same amp, you really want dedicated channels for each job – front component speakers and a single sub. A system like this, made up from the right gear and fitted correctly, can sound awesome. If you want it to sound great and go realistically loud, you'll do just fine with some five- or six-in components.

You can hear this KISS thing do a stonking job at Sound Offs all over the world – and with many different brands of equipment. So don't think that just because one make seems to crop up in magazines all the time, or because you hear everyone raving about it, that it's the only thing you should consider.

Good installation is probably 75 per cent of the finished sound, so getting the gear bolted into your car correctly will improve the final performance more than just buying something more expensive. But when you do a mega installation, you can start looking at mega equipment, knowing that you're going to be able to get the last gram of performance from it because the install's top-notch.

To get a lot more output from your system – that is, you want your car to be very loud – the easiest way is to start doubling up on your gear. Two pairs of component drivers fitted in the front of the car and multiple sub woofers will let you really build the pressure up while keeping things worth listening to. If you start loading your back shelf down with lots of different speakers wired up to your head unit, you're just wasting your money and your dealer's time. It isn't going to get really loud or sound any good, and you're going to wonder why all that equipment isn't doing the job you want.

As your demands and expectations rise, you can add other items such as outboard active crossovers and equalisers. You'll probably need the advice of a good dealer who really knows how to get the best out of them before you go spending your hard-earned dosh, though, otherwise you might end up with some impressive-looking boxes that aren't really doing their stuff.

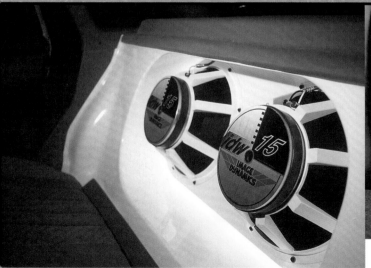

Basically speaking

Preparing a vehicle for a decent installation will help you do the job better, carry it out faster and give you a better finished result. I'm talking about removing enough panels, seats and carpeting so you can do what you need to, without breaking anything as you try to force your way past the one thing you didn't remove.

If you have to run several cables the length of the car, whip a seat out and lift the carpet rather than struggling like an idiot. It is not big or clever to try to feed the cables under the carpet while the seat's still holding it roughly in place – you'll probably rip your arms to shreds on the sharp bits of steel on the floor and it will definitely take longer to do.

If you're adding quite a bit of equipment, don't just rush at fitting one thing. You may find you've got to take half the car apart again to run the wiring that you forgot to put in while it was still in pieces. Instead, plan what you need to do by looking at where you're going to fit things, and then thinking about how to wire them up. We'll tackle some wiring stuff first, then move on to basic preparation, including sound deadening.

There are a few rules for laying out the cabling. Stick to them when you plan the wire runs and you shouldn't have any problems. The main thing is to keep the car stereo wiring as far away as possible from the vehicle wiring, particularly if the car has airbags and seatbelt tensioners. These things are explosive, so you don't want to trigger them accidentally. It can be painful, to your body and your wallet.

When you lift a piece of your carpet, find the original vehicle wiring loom and look where it runs in relation to where you want your wiring to go. The most important wire that you have to

run is the signal cable, which goes between your head unit and the rest of the system. It carries low-level signal that can easily be polluted by electrical noise from other vehicle systems, so it needs to be away from as much car wiring as possible.

Invariably, though, you'll find a place where the signal cable passes over, or close to, a vehicle loom. If it must run alongside, make it happen for the shortest length possible. If they have to cross over each other, try to lay them out so they cross at right angles. Doing this will minimise the chances of interference getting into the system at an early stage.

If it seems logical and the cable runs are well away from vehicle wiring – and from each other – go ahead. If not, maybe you need to reconsider how your install should be laid out.

And when you're running signal cables, be prepared to split them up to make the job easier. Signal cables are usually made up of two side-by-side conductors. So while it's easy enough to run them over a lumpy floor, it can be difficult to make them lay flat when they go round a corner. If you pull the two cables apart, though, you can lay them alongside each other and then stick them in place with gaffa tape. It will look the same when you get to the amp rack because you'll probably split them there anyway, so you might as well make things easier while you're under the carpet.

The last couple of things to suss are relays and diodes. They are both incredibly useful, and once you've figured out what they do and how they can help you, you'll use them all the time. Well, that's a bit of an exaggeration, but you'll use them occasionally and you'll be glad you did.

Put very simply, a relay is a switch. Sometimes it's an on/off switch, other times it's an A/B switch, and it might even be a timed delay switch, but whatever it does, it's just a switch. The reason you need relays in vehicle systems is because they can handle more current than the type of switch located on a dashboard.

When you turn on your heated rear window, all you're doing is making a remote relay pass the current to the window element. That's why you might hear a click from somewhere under the dash when you push the button. The click will be the large, sprung-loaded contact making the high-current circuit.

So why do you need a relay in a car stereo system? Well, the most common use is to switch on multiple components from the remote output of the head unit. Although it isn't often mentioned, a head unit has only a small output capability going down the remote wire, and if you have a few amps, an equaliser, a crossover and some cooling fans, you might be pushing your luck asking to turn them all on. Get your CD player to trip a relay instead and you can hang loads of components on the end of it without danger of burning out your head unit.

As for diodes, just think of them as electrical one-way valves. While they are more often used in vehicle security installation, they do have occasional uses in car stereo. This might be an application where two items fed power to one point under different circumstances, but they needed to be protected from one another.

For example, let's say you have a separate radio/cassette and a MiniDisc player, and they both feed into your system through a switching box. It sounds unlikely, but there are systems like this. You need both units to be able to turn on the rest of the amps and crossover, but only one at a time. If you put a diode into each remote-output line from the two source units, you won't get a possibly damaging back-feed entering the unit that's turned off when you turn the other one on.

It's the relay thing

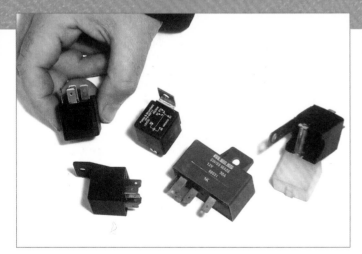

Here's a selection of relays, including one with a built-in fuse to protect the item being switched. The big blue one is a central door locking relay that handles the current for popping door locks.

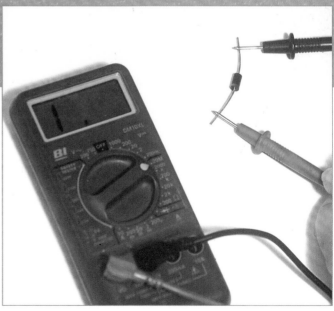

This shows a diode passing current (top) and blocking it (bottom). Diodes are really useful in many areas of electrical installation, and you can use them as a one-way valve.

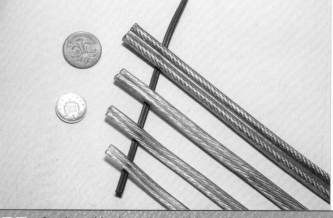

A few ideas

01 Clockwise from the thinnest wire, we've got 8-gauge, 4-gauge, 2-gauge and 0-gauge. It's weird, but the smallest number is the biggest cable. The thinnest stuff shown is typical low-power wire. Cable sizes can go up to 0000-gauge, but that's so thick you probably couldn't bend it without motorised help. And it isn't designed for in-car use.

Basic wiring crimp terminals are colour-coded according to what wire size they'll accept. The red-bodied terminals will accept normal vehicle wiring without any trouble, but once you get onto slightly thicker cables, you move up to blue or yellow terminals. If you try to use a terminal that's too big for the wire you're working with, you might find it just falls off, even when you've really leaned on the crimping pliers.

03

02 Speaker cable also varies in thickness depending on the job it's going to do. Big amps feeding big speakers need the heavy-duty stuff, but a noticeable gain in quality can be had from changing the standard cable to a decent quality one when you upgrade your speakers or add a small power amp. The factory-grade cable is the thinnest again, running under the better quality ones.

Cables and terminals

Car audio installations can use some pretty heavy-duty cables to pass the large amounts of current needed by big amps and the speakers they're powering. To give you an idea of the relative sizes of power wiring, here's a selection of the most popular ones, with a couple of coins as reference points.

For a decent quality install, you really need to use gold-plated connectors to keep the best conductivity throughout the system. These ring and fork terminals are for use on several different sizes of power and speaker cable, but the strange thing in the middle is a bolt-down earth connector. Fasten this to a good chassis earth and you should have no trouble with grounding your equipment.

04

Soldering on

There are some basic techniques you'll need to master if you want to get good results. Also, you'll need some useful bits in your workshop to do the job safely and more easily. Basic soldering is pretty easy, so let's start with a simple butt joint to see how to do it properly.

01 The first job is to prepare the two wires you need to join. Strip about 15mm of insulation from each of them.

02 Then slip the heatshrink tubing into place so you can cover the joint later.

03 The two ends need twisting together to give a good mechanical joint before any solder works its way in.

04 Now for the tricky stuff. Apply a dab of solder to the hot iron tip and when it's melted, wipe it away on the bit cleaning sponge to clean the tip of the iron. You have to keep burnt resin and contaminants off the iron or your joints won't last as long as they otherwise would.

Then dab some more solder on the clean tip and put this against the joint area. After a few seconds, you should be able to put some solder against the iron tip and watch it flow into the hot joint. If the joint isn't hot enough, the solder will sit on the iron until the heat has worked through the joint. It will also have worked through the insulation to your fingers, so either hold the wire a long way from the joint or hold with something like a pair of pliers.

05 What you want to see is a nice, smooth, solid joint like this. The solder has flooded into the strands of wire, making the join very solid indeed.

06 Now the heatshrink tube is brought up to cover the joint and it gets a quick blast of hot air from a heat gun. Once it's shrunk down, the joint is safe as well as strong. Job done.

Tee time

Joining a second wire on to an existing wire calls for a slightly different kind of join, but most of the technique's the same.

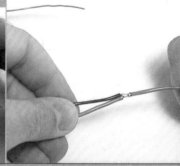

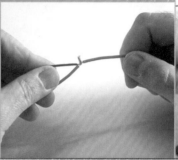

01 First, you need to bare a few millimetres of the existing wire with some wire strippers or a sharp knife. Be careful not to cut the strands of wire, though.

02 The second wire should be wrapped tightly around the exposed wire to give another good mechanical joint.

03 Once the solder has been applied and you have a smooth join, it will look like this. Note how the joining cable has been laid against the other one to make insulating the join neater.

Testing time

Here's a neat test of your soldering ability that also makes a useful tool. A speaker battery can be used to check wiring and speaker polarity. The idea is that when you touch the terminal of a battery against the terminals of a speaker, it will make a crackling noise and you can see the cone move either in or out.

If you touch the battery positive wire to the speaker positive terminal (and the battery negative wire to the speaker negative terminal), the cone moves outwards – remember 'like poles repel' from your physics lessons? When you reverse the wires, the cone is pulled towards the magnet because opposite poles attract. It's very useful for testing which way a speaker's been wired when you've run your cable but can't see the positive tracer any more, or you can't remember which way round you wired it.

Cool looms

04 Because we couldn't get heatshrink on to the main wire, we have to wrap the joint in insulating tape. Make sure the joint is smooth so that no stray pieces of wire poke through the tape. If they do, they may short out and cause problems later.

01 If you've ever wondered how those neat twisted wiring looms are made, this is how. You just need a battery drill and your wire. Cut the wires you're going to loom together a bit longer than you need, because the twisting process shortens them a little. Then just insert one lot of wire ends into the drill chuck and tighten it up. Keep the other ends held tightly during the process, preferably with some pliers rather than your fingers.

02 Now pull the trigger and watch the loom form before your very eyes. Cool! You can loom lots of wires this way, but you have to be careful that they all stay in the chuck while they're spinning. If one comes out, you'll end up with a messy loom that you should really do again.

01 We used a 1.5-volt AAA battery and twisted a few inches of wire so that it fitted over the battery length like this. Then we cleaned the battery terminals with some emery paper to give a keyed surface for the solder to run into.

02 The terminals were heated and tinned, which means a coating of solder was melted on to them, ready for the joint.

03 After tinning the wire ends, the wire was joined on to the battery terminals at each end. Simple.

04 The final job was to wrap the battery up in tape to stop any unwanted shorting-out and to provide a bit of strain relief for the wiring. We used yellow as the live wire, just to be different, but kept black as the negative wire because we didn't want anyone getting it mixed up. And that's it. A five-minute job that makes a really useful tool.

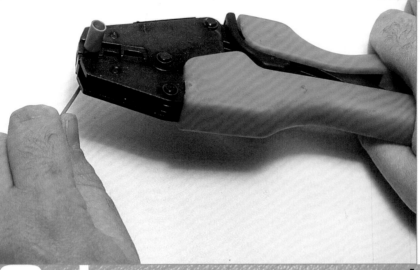

01 These ratchet crimping pliers make the job very easy. They are so long you get good leverage on the terminal and it doesn't take much effort to squeeze it on to the wire. They're great when you have a lot of terminals to put on.

Crimp your style

When you don't want to solder a joint, crimped terminals are a very good option. So long as they are the right size and joined correctly on to the wire, they'll never come off unless pulled extremely hard. They make a good contact, too. Here we'll show you a couple of types of crimping tool and the results they produce.

In fact, one squeeze does two crimp lines and gives a very solid join. The only problem is that these pliers are quite expensive. If you are going to do a lot of crimping, though, they're worth the money.

02

These manual crimps are more the thing for occasional use, but they can still do a good job. Grip the terminal in the correct section of the jaws and a couple of squeezes makes a neat join.

03

The finished result is just as strong as with the ratchet crimpers, but a bit more effort was required. It doesn't matter which type you choose. But make sure you use crimping pliers on crimp-fit terminals to get the most trouble-free performance.

04

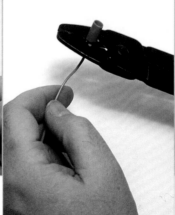

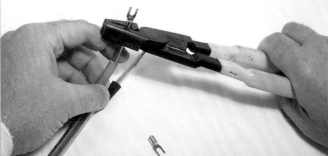

∧ **01** Tear the speaker wire apart to separate the two ends and make them easier to deal with. Then pull away the centre strip if your wire has one.

02 Don't forget to slip the heatshrink tubing on before you fit the terminals – otherwise you might not be able to squeeze it on once you've crimped them into place. The strange jaw shape on these pliers gives the perfect 'crimped up and rolled over' join needed to hold on to the cable incredibly tightly. Just what we need.

And here's two we did earlier. This method of terminating looks very cool and should be used if you're doing a flashy install so that you can show it off. These terminals look good when hooked up to amps, crossovers, processors, you name it. And with the right pliers, the joint is so tough you don't need to solder it.

A quick blast from the heat gun shrinks the insulation into place for a neat and tidy finish. **03**

04

Gold crimper

Crimping gold terminals on to thicker cable needs different pliers, but this is how to get a good joint if you splash out and buy the right tool for the job. Some designs of ordinary crimping pliers have a section that will give the same results, so check out your pliers before you spend the dosh.

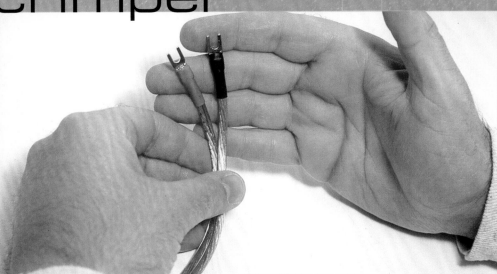

01 To get this Autoleads RCA plug on to its triple-screened signal cable, first split the plug into the inner and outer halves by unscrewing them. Then before doing anything else, slide the plug cover on to the RCA cable. Forget to do this now and you'll probably end up soldering the plug on before realising the cover is still on the bench – and then you'll have to start again. It's the kind of thing you do only once.

Sparkling **plugs**

This next job is a real test of your soldering abilities. Getting RCA signal plugs correctly fitted is an absolute must, so if you are unsure of your iron-wielding, buy ready-made leads and save yourself any grief. If you are confident you can solder neatly and correctly, carry on. Custom-made RCA cables are better because they are exactly the right length for the job and they are much neater to use because of it.

This is the slightly fiddly bit. The outer screen tail has to be threaded through the hole in the plug body while the centre conductor slips into the centre pin. Take care to get all the relevant strands of copper in the correct holes, and make sure there's no way that **05** anything can short out these two connectors.

This is how it should look when you're ready to get the iron going. Both tails have gone into the correct parts of the plug and the strain relief has been tightened up **06** with a careful nip from a pair of pliers.

Using a pair of large pliers as a makeshift vice to support the cable, the soldering iron can work on the centre pin easily. Again, we had to wait for the iron to heat up the wire and the pin so that the solder flowed into the joint and made a **07** smooth bond over the two parts.

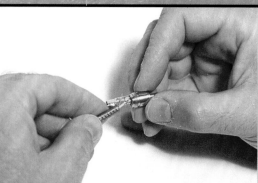

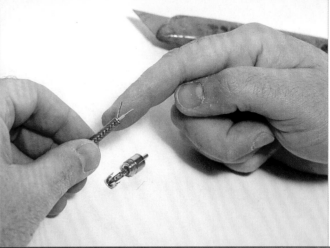

02 The cable preparation begins by removing the outer layer of insulator and the first two screens, which are braided copper and foil sheet. Gently and carefully cut them away to get to the next insulation layer.

03 Once you've got the next insulator out of the way, the second braided-copper screen should be twisted into a tail like this, ready for soldering into the RCA plug.

04 Now you can see the centre conductor has been uncovered and twisted before adding the plug.

Now it's the turn of the outer screen to be joined to the outside of the plug. Keep this join very neat because the plug cover has to slide over it before it can screw down tight. If it's too lumpy, the cover **08** won't sit in place.

Nearly finished. You can see how the solder has flowed over the back of the plug to give a solid join and how neat and blob-free the **09** centre pin is.

And here's the finished item. The cover has been screwed into place and the joint is protected. It takes a few minutes to do one of these joints properly. If you have a lot to do, ready-made cables can seem like an easier bet, **10** but doing your own cables is far neater.

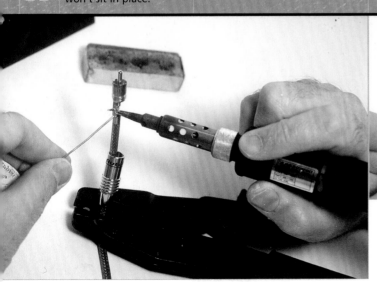

Powering up

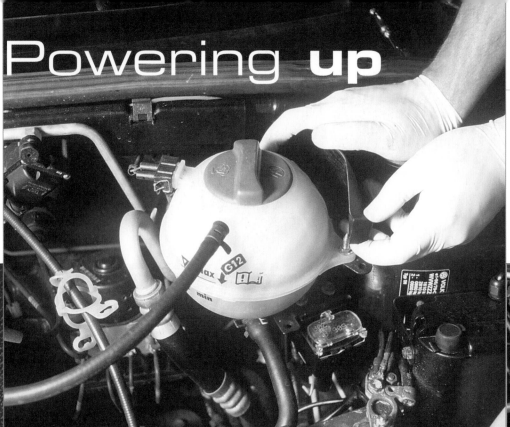

01 The grommet we're going to use is hidden behind the radiator expansion bottle, so first we have to remove the bolt cover.

Once that's done, we can undo the bolts and gently lean the bottle out of the way. **02**

How do you get a thumping great power cable through from the engine bay to the passenger compartment? To show you, we've added some nice thick 4-gauge wire to a MkIII Golf. Here's what we did.

07 Back at the car, we've fed a thinner piece of cable through the bulkhead hole to act as a 'mouse wire'. This will help us pull the power cable through when we're ready.

08 We've taped the end of the power cable on to the mouse, using it to pull the thicker wire gently into the car.

09 It helps to have someone guiding the cable into the hole under the bonnet while you're pulling from the other side.

10 Having figured out roughly where the grommet will sit on the power cable when it's fully installed, we put a good run of tape over the nose of the cable grommet to make absolutely sure it stays watertight.

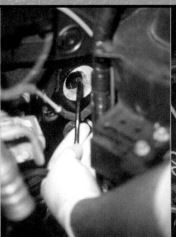

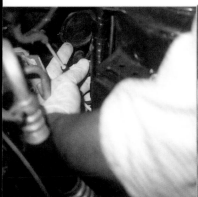

03 That's where we're heading. This big plastic grommet is an easy way into the car for our power cable.

04 Once the grommet's removed, you can see the hole in the under-carpet insulation on the other side of the bulkhead.

05 Here's the VW factory grommet, with the power cable grommet we're going to use, and our secret weapon – the geasket cutter.

Once we've thumped the grommet with the gasket cutter, we're left with a small but perfectly formed hole, ready for the cable grommet.

06 Here we've assembled the cable grommet through the factory grommet and put a piece of 4-gauge cable in so you can see how it's going to look.

11 Now all we have to do is wriggle the factory grommet back into place.

12 You can see we've covered the power cable with convoluted tube to protect it, and we've added the all-important fuse holder, which needs to be as close to the battery as you can get it.

13 Volkswagen's battery terminal, rather thoughtfully, has a nice threaded hole ready for a new bolt – ideal for attaching the amp power wire.

14 We put the expansion bottle back on, with the new power cable in place, looking pretty factory.

To remove a door panel, you'll probably have to hunt round for hidden screws and fasteners. The door pull on our Honda CRX has a screw hidden away in it.

01

There's also a Phillips screw tucked round the back of the electric window switch module that needs rooting out before we can unclip it from the door.

02

Kill the noise

A few ideas

Before we can sound deaden any of the vehicle's metalwork, we have to get to it. And once we've got to it, we need to clean it. This is what you do.

Now we unclipped the electric window and mirror wiring from the inner doorskin, before removing the vapour barrier.

07

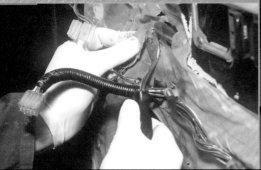

In some areas, the adhesive had gone hard and needed warming up with a hot-air gun before it would move. We also used thinners on a rag to polish the last bits of goo out of the way.

11

Finally, we could install the vapour barrier in the same place as that duff speaker.

09

The doorskin needed some serious cleaning. Here we've used a piece of scrap MDF to remove the sticky adhesive that held the vapour barrier in place.

10

The last thing to come off was the door pull support.

08

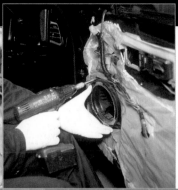

03 Once we'd pulled the module from the door, we had to unplug it gently from the wiring loom.

04 One of these crow-footed panel lifters can help get the door trim off without breaking any of the clips that hold it in place.

05 Having removed the trim panel, we found this rather ropy old speaker that didn't really fit properly. So we binned it.

06 The next thing to come off was the speaker holder, which just needed unscrewing.

With the inner door panel finally cleaned off, we removed any little bits that would get in the way when rollering the deadening sheet **12** into place.

The first piece of Dynamat Extreme going on. We used a hardwood wallpaper edge-roller to work it into every crease and ripple of the inner doorskin. Notice the slit we've made, halfway down **13** the sheet, for the wiring loom.

With the sheet firmly stuck in place, chop out the hole where the speaker should be going. This is done with a sharp craft knife. You can see that the wiring loom we cut the **14** slit for is now back in its normal position.

15 Here's the finished inner door skin, with the first of the speaker mounting clips uncovered. Once you've rollered the sheet into place, you'll be able to see things like this under the surface. Then you can cut the small pieces of sheet out of the way so that you can reuse them when you re-fit the door furniture.

Simple stuff

Okay, enough of the theory. Let's get stuck in to some real jobs. We'll get started with the easier stuff. These are worthwhile jobs that give a sizeable increase in performance for the small amount of effort involved.

On most modern cars, the manufacturer-supplied head unit probably looks the business, but underneath that neat facia is almost certainly a rather under-whelming set. Couple that to the cheapest speakers they could reasonably get away with, and you've hardly got a recipe for killer sound.

Even with the bargain-basement speakers, it's still worth changing to a more sophisticated head unit, because the better and more powerful the signal going into the speakers, the better they'll sound. Most aftermarket head units are now producing reasonable power outputs, so they'll drive factory speakers harder and with less distortion.

If yours is an upmarket motor, don't think that the factory set-up is necessarily good. Even cars costing megabucks scrimp when it comes to the music. Without mentioning any names, we know of one car that costs more than £100,000 – it's German, has four doors, and a V12 engine – yet the quality of the components in its supposedly top-flight all-singing, all-dancing digital ICE system were noted in an electronics catalogue as merely 'suitable for low-cost consumer electronics'. Hardly high fidelity.

If you're wondering why a manufacturer would scrimp and save on the stereo system, ask yourself one question. Do you think the stereo is the real reason that someone buys a new car? Absolutely not. Performance, economy, comfort, handling, looks, colour and many other things will be higher up the list of important things. All a car maker has to do is compete with the spec of a stereo from another manufacturer, so sounding good isn't generally a high priority.

If that argument hasn't convinced you, and you still want to keep your original head unit, help is still at hand. Most amplifiers allow you to feed their input stage with a high-level signal. If your chosen amp doesn't do that, there are adapters to ease the pain. This means that you can hook up your amp to the speaker outputs from the stereo without overloading anything or doing any damage.

As a result, you can put almost any type of system on the back of the stock head unit. So if you're really happy with your car's original CD player, you can still get a decent system going without swapping it. This is always assuming that you have a CD player in there, since amping up an original cassette player is a scary – and very probably time-wasting – proposition.

If you're worried that nothing else will fit in the possibly odd-shaped space of your existing head unit, fret no more. Companies like Autoleads do a wide range of adapter brackets that allow a standard DIN-sized stereo to be fitted into almost any weird manufacturer opening, so have a quick check down at your car stereo specialist to see what's available.

Just one thing. If you decide to build a system on the back of the standard head unit, at least try an aftermarket CD player in its place once you've got the rest of the gear fitted. If it sounds no better than the one that came with the car, fine. You've got really lucky. If the new one sounds better, though, at least you know where the next improvement's coming from – and where your next wage packet's going.

Almost regardless of your car, if you need an ISO adapter plug to fit your new unit, there will probably be one available to save you having to cut any wiring.

You should be able to get hold of the necessary adapter panels for your car, even if it has an oddly-shaped head unit or weird-looking speakers.

The CD-45z is a great match for the Golf's cosmetics and looks really at home in the dash. The small knob to the right of it is the bass level control that's supplied with the Caliber active crossover, and another of our little additions.

Simple stuff

Straightforward
head unit swap

To prove how weedy original head units are, we decided to ditch the one fitted to this MkIII VW Golf GTI. Although it wasn't the factory-fitted unit, we whipped it out before taking any photos to save the radio manufacturer's embarrassment. The replacement unit was going to be a straightforward installation, but we were adding it along with a few other goodies to make the Golf sound significantly better.

Even though the set we took out was a very similar model to the original unit, someone had still managed to do a bit of hacking to the wiring behind it. This is one of the pitfalls of doing work after someone else has already been in there, but at least head unit wiring shouldn't cause too many problems, regardless of how badly it's been butchered.

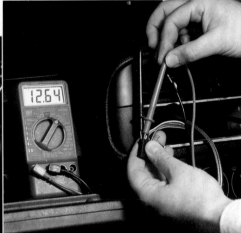

01 With the removed set already winging its way to the scrap pile, the mounting sleeve for the Nakamichi CD player was secured in position by bending the lugs over in the Golf's dash aperture.

02 Here's the sleeve in position, and the wiring ready to be terminated to match up to the Nakamichi's outputs.

03 A quick check with the multimeter showed which wires were needed for the new set. Thankfully they hadn't been too badly butchered by the ham-fisted person who'd been into the dash before us.

04 Crimping the new terminals on to the VW's head unit feeds made for simple connections, so there was no need for an adapter. The Nakamichi doesn't use an ISO connector, so we just took the ISO plug off the Golf and fitted bullets instead. You wouldn't want to do this on a brand new car that's still under warranty, but the Golf was old enough for it not to be an issue.

05 This was a lot neater than the stuff that came out on the old unit. All we needed to do now was fit the RCA plugs to the purple wire you can see hanging out of the hole.

06 Here's the final wiring assembly, just before it was pushed back into the dash. We connected only one of the Nakamichi's outputs because the system wasn't running rear speakers.

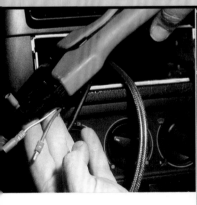

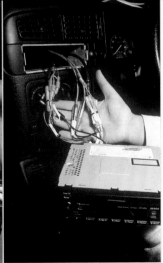

Speakers

01 The MkIII Golf's door allocations take a 165mm speaker, which is hidden behind a plastic grille. Getting the grille out of the way requires a quick flick of a narrow pick or screwdriver under its lower edge, like this.

Even now that good speakers aren't so expensive, motor manufacturers still penny-pinch on them because a penny saved is a few thousand quid more profit when you're making a shed-load of cars.

But this is easily solved. Decent speakers come in enough sizes and designs to fit right into the factory mounting, so you can upgrade your sounds without anyone knowing. If you want to go stealthily with your tunes, read on.

Door speakers – straight replacement

The easiest way to improve your car's sound quality is to fit something better into the original locations provided by the manufacturer. Trouble is, it isn't always that simple. There are cases when the best speakers in the world aren't really going to give you much benefit, so you need to know when to say forget it, and either go for improving the speakers and the location or making a completely new one.

Some cars have a very small standard speaker fitment, such as the MkII Golf, which has an 87mm dash-mounted driver. Other cars have very flimsy speaker mountings, such as the plastic dash grilles on Vauxhall Novas. If this is the case, there's no point in fitting anything spectacular there. If, on the other hand, you have something with a decent driver size and a solid place to put it, go ahead and take the easy option. It'll work nicely.

To prove this, we swapped the door and dash speakers in a MkIII Golf GTi from the original under-achievers to some MB Quart components to show how easy it is.

02 Now that we can get to it, we can unscrew the speaker and save it for when the car is sold.

03 The plastic terminal block is wriggled free from the driver, and then we're ready to remove the tweeter from the dash.

04 The tweeter grille comes off as easily as the door grille, just needing a flick of a panel tool to flip it out of the way.

05 The large tweeter is also clipped in position and is soon on its way to join the door speaker.

Now we need to cut off the terminal block and fit some proper fork terminals to attach to the speakers.

06

The terminals are crimped in position and then covered with heatshrink for protection and colour coding – red for positive, black for negative.

07

Then they are screwed on to the Quart mid range.

08

Finally the speaker is screwed back into the door panel and the grille is clipped back. No one will be the wiser until they listen to the much-improved sound.

09 >

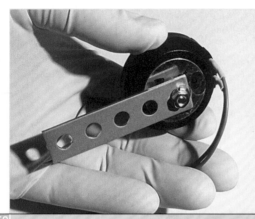

10 The MB Quart tweeter is simply bolted to a piece of strip bracket that is going to be screwed into the dash.

11 The tweeter is quite small, but the sound will far outstrip the standard offering.

12 To smarten up the mounting strip, it's covered in black heatshrink tubing.

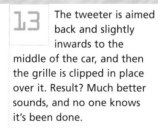

13 The tweeter is aimed back and slightly inwards to the middle of the car, and then the grille is clipped in place over it. Result? Much better sounds, and no one knows it's been done.

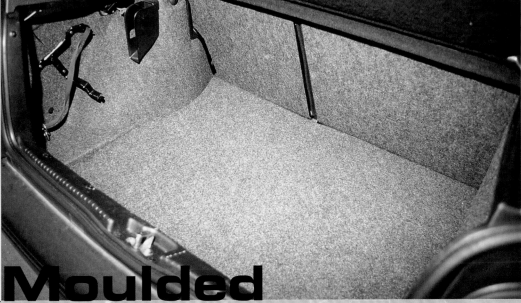

Moulded glass fibre sub box

Having sorted the Golf's front speakers, we couldn't leave it bass-less. But we didn't want to drop in a big, cabinet that would take up half the boot. The solution we came up with was a ready-made enclosure from Audioscape.

This glass fibre cabinet is moulded around the wheelarch of the Golf's boot area, taking up very little boot floor area but giving a nice solid enclosure of just under one cubic foot. This was about right to take a JL Audio 10W0 sub woofer and let it perform perfectly happily.

01 This is the boot before we started filling it up with gear. All we had to remove was the triangle holder and the First Aid kit holder. Neither was in active use, so that wasn't a big deal.

02 This is the bare Audioscape box, from the front and the back. Notice that it has a nice curvy front, and look how complicated that rear side is. It really maximises use of the space under the shelf support.

> **Achtung!**
> *MDF dust is nasty stuff to breathe in. Wear a mask when you're cutting, drilling or sanding it.*

After marking the outline, we drilled a couple of pilot holes to get the jigsaw blade into **04** the box.

It was a good job we had a sharp jigsaw blade. The glass fibre baffle was backed by an MDF ring to make sure that the woofer would screw in rock solid **05** and prevent air leaks.

03 The first job was to cut out the 232mm woofer mounting hole in the cabinet, being very careful not to mark any of the smooth speaker baffle. Audioscape will cut the hole for you if you give them the size you need when you order it, but we did the job ourselves.

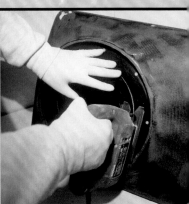

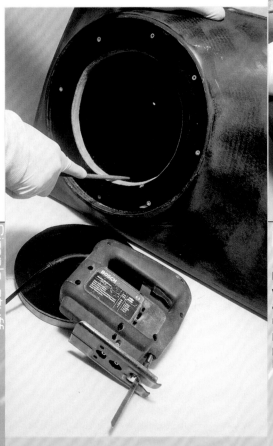

06 Once the hole was cut out, we used a round file to knock off any high spots that stopped the woofer from fitting. You should always try to cut a woofer mounting hole as snugly as possible to give the speaker plenty of support and stop air leakage.

07 After trial-fitting the woofer a few times, we were happy that it was a good enough fit. It even held itself in place for the photo.

We soldered the wires on to the sub and left enough wire spare so we could remove the woofer easily, should we need to. The box bolts in by one nut, which fits through the back of the box. That means the woofer needs to come out if we have to remove the box, hence the long lead.

Finally, we could cut the carpet from around the woofer opening and then push it back into the corner of the lip that surrounds the baffle.

12

This is the box with the grille test-fitted in position to make sure it's okay after trimming. It looked fine to us.

13

14

08 This is a very delicate exercise. Drilling the speaker screw holes should be done carefully so that there's no chance of slipping and damaging the speaker cone. We drilled all eight holes out to make sure the woofer stayed put. If you're nervous about doing this, mark the holes and remove the speaker before you drill them.

09 Now we could trim the front of the box in some flecked grey carpet that matched the VW stuff quite closely. We started by cutting out a piece a few inches bigger than the face of the box.

10 We masked off the speaker baffle, then glued the front of the box and the back of the carpet. To get a good bond, the contact adhesive needs to go tacky before both bits are brought together.

11 The carpet was pulled and stretched across the face of the box to get it nice and smooth, then heaved round the corners to keep it taut.

We even used heatshrink on the terminals and cable-tied the wire to the magnet to stop any possible problems, should the woofer ever be removed.

15

The final job before screwing the sub in place was to fill the enclosure with wadding. This helps the woofer's performance. You can either use proper speaker wadding, which can be expensive and difficult to get, or polyfill from a dressmaking shop. They use it for stuffing toys and quilts.

16

The finished result looks the part, sounds great and doesn't take up much space. And the sub does kick like a mule when required, which proves it's in the right size of box.

17

Shelve it

A common way to get bigger and better speakers into a hatchback is to fit them into the parcel shelf. Now, we aren't saying that this is the best place to fit new speakers. In fact, many decent-sounding systems don't have any speakers in the back at all. But given that a lot of people are going to drop some thumpers into a shelf, it might as well be done right.

01 This is the full kit before we got going with our jigsaw, paint and carpet glue.

Simple stuff

To demonstrate what goes into the job, we got hold of an Auto Acoustics Stealth Shelf, which, when it's made up and finished, looks almost identical to the original factory one.

So why don't we just chop a couple of holes out of the shelf that the manufacturer has fitted? There are a couple of good reasons. The main one is weight – a factory shelf is normally so soft and flimsy that it would collapse after a few weeks with a couple of decent speakers in it.

This looks awful, and sounds even worse. All speakers have to be mounted solidly or they just won't perform properly, so a solid shelf is vital.

The other reason will become clear when you sell the car. If you stick good speakers into a standard shelf, you have two main options when you sell it. Either you leave your speakers in there and lose them or you take them out and leave stonking great ugly holes in the shelf. By fitting the speakers in an aftermarket shelf, you get better sound and can save the original shelf for resale time.

There's one small point to remember with these MDF replacement shelves – they're quite a bit heavier than the original chewed-paper items that come from the factory. If you go for this type of speaker install, make sure you have a good go at fastening your shelf down with something a bit more solid than the plastic pins that are screwed on to their front corners.

To prove it isn't a big job, here's how we fitted some Velocity 6x9s into a Fiat Punto Stealth Shelf.

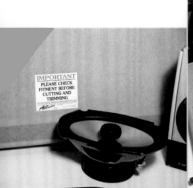

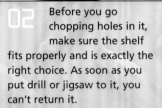

02 Before you go chopping holes in it, make sure the shelf fits properly and is exactly the right choice. As soon as you put drill or jigsaw to it, you can't return it.

03 Once we'd decided where we wanted the speakers to go, we measured them from the shelf ends and front edge to get them symmetrical. The plan was for the cone to appear just inside the lip of the top of the shelf.

04 After marking the screw hole positions using the speaker ring, they were drilled through the MDF to show us where to put the ring on the underside of the shelf.

05 Flipping the shelf over meant it was easy to line up the speaker ring on the holes we'd drilled from the top, giving us the exact position of the area to be cut out.

Achtung!
MDF dust is nasty stuff to breathe in. Wear a mask when you're cutting, drilling or sanding it.

Still working on the underneath, we cut out the holes with a jigsaw, following the inside of the line we'd drawn using the speaker ring template.

06

After all the drilling and cutting, the underside of the shelf was sprayed black to smarten up its appearance. Notice what a good impromptu spray booth the Auto Acoustics packaging made – perfect for keeping the garage wall clean.

07

Back on the top side, two pieces of grille cloth were stretched and stapled across the speaker hole. This was done to prevent the carpet from sagging over time. If any staples didn't quite go all the way in, they were belted with a hammer to flatten them fully.

08

After the cloth was stretched out and stapled, the baggy offcuts were removed. Then the shelf was ready for gluing and covering.

09 >

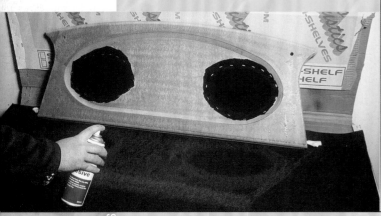

10 By standing the shelf on its edge on the underside of the carpet, both surfaces can be sprayed with glue. Leave a couple of areas of the carpet unglued where the speakers will play through.

11 The edge of the shelf and the carpet were sprayed to give a good bond with a very solid hold and no chance of coming loose.

12 The corners proved easier to trim than we'd thought, even though they were a funny shape to wrap with carpet. The masking tape stopped the glue from going where it shouldn't and then peeled right off to leave an untouched shelf underneath.

17 These small ferrules made a good connection in the Neutrik speaker connector that terminated the shelf cabling.

18 We held the ferrules in place with a good dollop of solder, making sure that it flowed down inside the body of the ferrule and got a tight grip on the strands of cable.

19 Once they'd been soldered in position, the ends were pushed into the Neutrik plug assembly, according to the small symbols raised in the moulded plug. Follow the symbols and your speakers will be wired up the right way, first time.

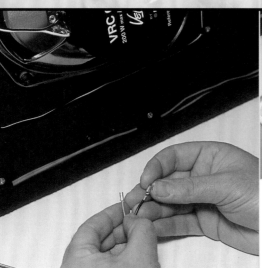
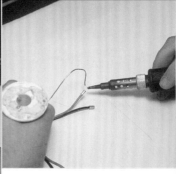
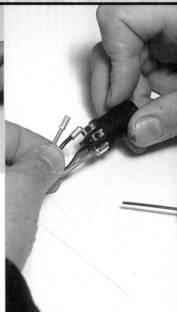

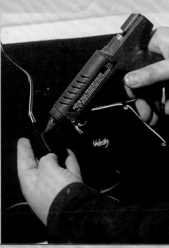

13 The speakers were screwed into the holes we drilled at the start of the project. There were terminals on both sides of the speaker, so it didn't really matter which way round they faced. In the end, we put the bigger bass terminals together because we wanted to fit the outboard passive crossover networks between the speakers for a bit of protection.

14 The crossovers were hot-glued to the centre of the shelf so that their wires could be laid out neatly to each speaker. When you are doing something like this, take a few more minutes to do it neatly. It looks better, makes you feel prouder of your work and is more likely to impress others.

15 We screwed the low-pass wires into these heavy-duty binding posts. A dab of solder on each wire made them strong enough to be really wound down on by the knurled collar.

16 Small P-clips kept the wires running where they should be. It will also stop them hanging down and getting ripped off the first time a bag of shopping is thrown into the boot.

20 The wiring was held in place by small Allen screws, which needed a good tightening to make the best electrical contact.

21 Here's the Neutrik plug, laid out before it's screwed together. A couple of keyways mean it can only be assembled the right way, so as long as you don't force the pieces together, you'll have a trouble-free quick-release shelf connector.

22 The opposing socket has four spade terminals on the back of it, so you can just crimp the wiring from the stereo to this. Once you've mounted the socket in the boot panelling, a pop-in, pop-out shelf is yours.

23 Here's the finished underside of the shelf, ready for action. But from the top, you'd never know it was any different from a standard shelf. Cool and clever.

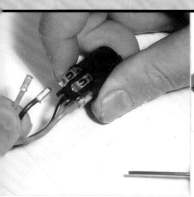

95

Screen test

Working out where to fit a TV screen in your motor can be a bit of a daunting prospect – particularly if it isn't obvious where you can stick it. And what do you do if the original location looks fine but isn't really suitable for a flip-out screen?

In a lot of cars, the main problem with a flip-up dash-mounted screen is that bits of the dash are obscured by the screen when it's out. Most vehicle manufacturers never intended a motorised screen to wind its way out of the original radio slot, so it's obvious they won't have allowed for the fact that it might cover up bits of kit. Sometimes it's just a couple of air vents that aren't that vital to the safe operation of the car, but sometimes a whole bank of switches disappears from view, and that can be a bit dodgy.

This was the case when we came to fit a flip-out TV in our Nissan 200SX. From the standard radio aperture, the screen would have covered the switches that controlled the rear fog light, heated rear window, hazard flashers and headlamp washers. Not the kinds of things you want to obsure, headlamp washer aside, perhaps. The whole of the heater panel would have gone, too.

Something had to be done, so we started taking things apart to see if we could drop the head unit down a bit further. This is what we found.

01 The easy first job is to take the console apart and get on with making a template for the replacement panel. We won't mention any names of the original unit we took out, but it wasn't doing a very good job. So it can wait in the bottom of a cupboard box until we sell the car and need it to fill the hole again.
The Nissan dash comes apart dead easily, with the top panel unclipping...

02 ...and then the gearlever surround following suit. That exposes five screws that hold the head unit bracket in place.

03 With those screws out of the way, the standard unit and small pocket fall out. They are held in an elaborate metal frame that screws on to the back of the plastic facia, and then into the dash itself. This cage arrangement supports the heavy radio a lot more solidly than the plastic trim could ever manage.

To get the stereo out, the wiring needs to be disconnected, leaving the unmolested Nissan **04** looms and plugs as they left the factory.

After taking the steel frame off the plastic dash piece, we put the facia back in place before checking that **05** the lower slot really won't do.

06 Nope, guess not. Sitting on the lower edge of the opening, the switches are totally blocked. Back to the drawing board.

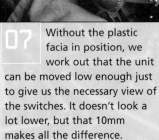
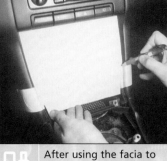

07 Without the plastic facia in position, we work out that the unit can be moved low enough just to give us the necessary view of the switches. It doesn't look a lot lower, but that 10mm makes all the difference.

08 After using the facia to draw this template, we check it for a decent fit. The tape marks on the console's side are the lowest point of the original opening, so we need to be 10mm lower than this.

09 This is the 9mm MDF panel that's going to be the new facia in about four hours.

Achtung!
MDF dust is nasty stuff to breathe in. Wear a mask when you're cutting, drilling or sanding it.

14 Here's a trial fit of the Alpine unit, and it looks pretty snug in its new home.

15 Happy that the panel is going to do its job, we set to filling in the screwheads and bevelling back the monitor unit mounting plate. Once the filler has gone off, we give it a quick rub down before sorting out the panel mounting brackets.

16 With the panel screwed back in place on its new brackets, we check the fit of the top and bottom dash pieces to see how much extra filling is needed.

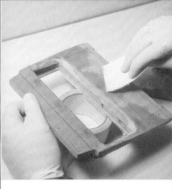

10 Having cut another piece of 9mm MDF to give the panel some thickness, we cut out the aperture large enough to go around the trim ring of the Alpine. Yes, that means it would fall through this panel, but you'll soon see why we've done this.

The top edge is perfect, but we need a little skim along the bottom edge to meet up neatly with the gearlever surround. After masking everything off in the area, we begin closing the gap with glass fibre filler paste. Plenty of care is taken to knock all the air bubbles out of the paste, and to get the contour as close as possible to what **17** we need. That gives us less sanding to do.

11 It's the only time you'll see us using a router in the book. There isn't any other way to get the nice bevelled edge we want around the radio hole, apart from sitting there and sanding the wood for about a week. If you do this kind of thing, get your local dealer to whip it round on his router table for you.

After the filler has gone off, we remove the panel and flip it over so you can see the brackets and the small spacer bar. This holds the DIN mounting-plate at a slight **18** angle to slant the nose of the unit down a little more.

12 This is the reason for routing the panel – that nice smooth edge.

Once the panel has been rubbed down a bit, we spray it with a guide coat of satin black paint. This makes it easier to find the high spots and low spots. Luckily for **19** us, there aren't many.

13 Next, we screw a universal DIN-plate to the back of the mounting panel to hold the Alpine monitor unit's DIN cage. The edges of the plate need chamfering in line with the new panel, otherwise the thing won't go into the Nissan dash.

Now it's a case of sanding away gently at the edges to get a perfect fit, taking into account that the panels are going to be trimmed with Alcantara **20** artificial suede.

>

21 Almost there. We've just got a couple of little high spots to knock off the panel, and it's ready for trimming.

22 During all this to-ing and fro-ing with panels, we've taken the time to finalise the position of the LPL-44 controller, which is hooked up to the Phoenix Gold equaliser in the back of the car. It's not strictly part of this install but we thought we'd show it now, so when you see the knob later, you'll know what it is.

23 Finally satisfied that the panel is sufficiently smooth and fits well enough, we cover it in spray glue and trim it with Alcantara. The nice easy shape isn't a bad job to do at all.

That must be one of the shortest RCA leads in history. The output from the Apline runs just over 30cm down to the input of the line driver. They do say you should keep the line driver as close as possible to the head unit, and you won't get it a lot closer than that. You can see that the rest of the wiring is neatly loomed up, and the redundant speaker wires are bagged up to keep them mint.

Here's the finished board and equipment mounted in place, showing how easy it is to get the necessary wiring out of the quarter panel and into the rest of the car.

Once everything's connected, you can see how the wiring runs across the back seat area, spread apart where possible, crossing at right-angles where unavoidable, and stuck down with gaffa tape all over the place. Now all we've got to do is put the side panel and rear seat back in.

28

29

30

24 With the DIN cage held firmly and the Alpine locked into it, we make a back bracket to support the unit. Rear supports are vital on CD players to keep them from wobbling about and tricking their internal suspension systems.

25 Having discounted the underdash and underseat areas as too small or too crowded to fit any extra gear, we try the passenger side rear quarter panel as a place for the Apline's brain and the Phoneix Gold PLD1 line driver. It looks like they'll fit, so we press on with part two of the scheme.

26 A mounting board is made from three pieces of 15mm MDF to hold the brain and the line driver as close together as possible, without hindering access to the line driver's gain control.

27 After checking the board is a good fit, we spray it black and let it dry before fitting and wiring up the brain and line driver.

It works. The screen comes out, the radio tunes in and the switches are still accessible. And that centre panel does look a lot more sexy than it used to. From this angle, you can't really tell that the switches are visible, but you can see what a nice fit the Apline is in the dash, and how discreet the LPL knob is as well.

31 Back at the dashboard, we couple up the monitor unit before slipping it back into place and reassembling the dash round it.

32 This is the only bit of the LPL control that sticks out from the gearlever surround, which has now been neatly trimmed to match the new monitor panel.

33

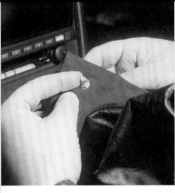

Headrest screen

With the front TV sorted out, we could have gone down the flash-rat route and gone for headrest screens as well. We didn't mainly because the rear seats are so tiny we couldn't get anyone in there with any comfort to watch them. Even so, we wanted to show you what goes into dropping a screen into a headrest.

To help us to find out the best way to get the job done, we stopped in at SQ Plus in Manchester, where Phil Leach was adding a pair of Alpine widescreen monitors into a BMW. Here's what we learnt.

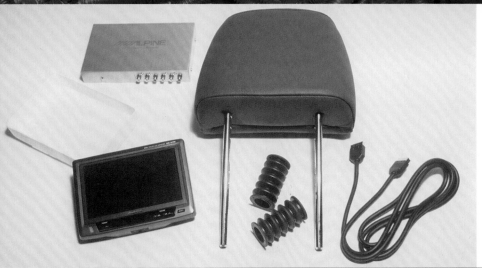

01 The unmolested headrest in place. It looks big enough for a widescreen Alpine monitor, so let's have a go at dropping one in.

02 Here's the gear we're going to use. There's the Alpine monitor, BMW headrest, monitor fitting box, monitor signal cable and a pair of rubber concertina grommets to cover the headrest legs once the cable is fitted.

The first job is to get the headrest in bits to see what lies under the outer trim. On the BMW headrest, the leather cover needs careful prising out of a long clip, which holds it taut over the foam liner. Most headrest covers are clipped together on their underside, between the support legs. A bit of gentle pulling about should show you how the **03** seam splits apart so that you can get the cover off.

Be especially careful when pulling the headrest apart because you can accidentally split the cover. The hard plastic shell isn't really any bigger than the hole in the cover. If you just heave on the cover to get it **04** off, don't be surprised if it rips. You've been warned.

Here we have the leather cover and foam insert separated from the plastic shell and support legs. The screen mounting box will be screwed to this plastic piece so **05** that the screen doesn't move around in the headrest.

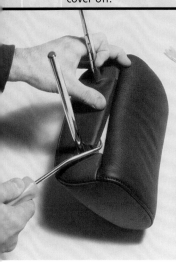

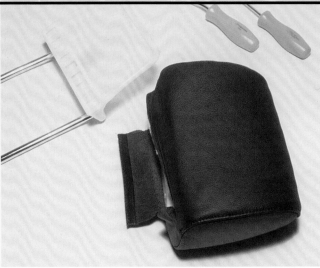

06 Careful squashing and pulling of the foam liner gets it out of the cover without any problems.

07 Once we have refitted the foam liner to the plastic support, we check the mounting box position. When happy with that, we draw a line around the screen box on the back of the foam liner. This part of the job is done with skill and experience rather than just measuring the box position. You often find that something might be correctly measured but looks wrong, whereas something that looks right, just looks right. No one will measure it if they think it's in the correct place.

08 After marking the foam, the hole is cut out with a very sharp craft knife. The sharp blade is the key to getting a nice smooth line without the foam cutting roughly along the edges.

09 We've split the foam and support so you can see just how big a hole is required for a widescreen monitor. Okay, let's put it back together again.

14 With the headrest assembly the other way round and the first small hole cut into the leather, small pieces of foam are added around the screen mounting-box. This is to pad out the edges and get a nice even look all the way round the monitor aperture.

15 The moment of truth. Satisfied that the box is correctly aligned, we have a go at chopping out the surplus leather, which would stop the screen going in neatly. A sharp knife cuts smoothly through the leather trim without causing any rips or rough edges.

16 After masking up the outside of the headrest, the leftover leather flaps can be glued down into the mounting box. This stops the leather working free once the car is being used again. The Autoleads spray glue is very effective for this job, going tacky in a few minutes and then grabbing on to the leather for good.

17 The next stage is to thread the monitor cable down through the box and out from the underside of the headrest. It should exit near a support leg so that it can be hidden away when it goes back into the car.

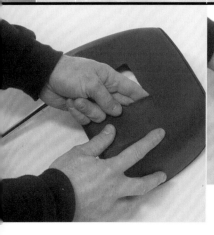

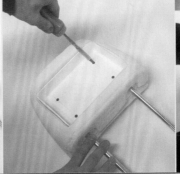

10 Now we can check the fit of the screen box in the hole in the foam, making sure it looks level from top-to-bottom, and centred from side-to-side. With it looking spot-on, we can get out the drill.

11 The box and headrest shell are drilled for the fixing screws. It's important to keep the box exactly lined up at this stage or it will be screwed in place at a slight angle and it will never look right once the cover is back on.

12 The box is screwed in place on the headrest, before being undone and removed for a test-fit in the foam and leather pad combination.

13 The box needs test-fitting to see whether or not any extra padding is required. This is to make the box look like it belongs in the headrest rather than being a poor addition.

The job's almost finished. The screen is a very snug fit so it probably wouldn't need anything else to hold it in safely. The careful prep work now shows because the monitor is bang in the middle and looks **18** just right.

These rubber door grommets cover the headrest legs and hide the wire away. They might look slightly odd when the headrest is out of the car, but once **19** they are refitted, they'll look fine.

This comparison shows how neat the new addition is, and how **20** factory it looks.

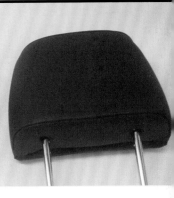

That isn't
where it normally goes

This is where it starts to get a bit more adventurous. We're going to be dealing with speakers and, more specifically, putting speakers in places where the car manufacturer never intended them to go. This is to get better performance from the speaker kit we'll be using.

So often, the original speaker location is chosen simply because it is easy to use on the production line. Very few vehicle manufacturers have got their heads around speaker placement for best audio performance yet, so these techniques will be valid for a good few years yet.

First, though, it's worth talking about sound, the way we hear it and the way to get the best results from the new gear we're fitting. Our ears and brains work best when sound arrives at our heads from in front of us. Over millions of years, our ears have developed to work with our eyes so that we can watch the world and listen to it as well. Of course, our ears pick up sound from all around us, but the design of our outer ear means we can tell if a sound is behind us. When that happens, we turn round to see what it is. It probably dates back to the time when if you didn't turn to look at what made the sound behind you, it ripped your head off and chewed you for a while.

Anyway, it stands to reason to try to get the music to arrive from the front. After all, if you see a band in concert you face the stage, and when you talk to someone, you generally face them as well. Club music is different because it hits you from all sides, but that isn't normally how music is played. So let's assume the music needs to be in front of our heads.

We've already looked at the straight swap of speakers in an earlier chapter, so let's get stuck into something that needs a bit more work. We'll start simply enough, but we've still got a good reason to get the jigsaw out and start chopping MDF.

Door speaker – making a mounting plate

In most cars we'd always recommend using the biggest size of driver you can fit – within reason – so that you get the best mid-bass response or 'kick' possible. But not every car will accept a better driver in the original size in the standard location.

Some large openings are restricted by the depth available behind the mounting. It isn't clever to fit a speaker only to find that your window clunks into the magnet before you've wound it fully down. So what options do you have when the straight swap isn't that straightforward?

So long as you are fitting a high-quality speaker, you always have the option of using a slightly smaller driver that actually fits. To show you what we mean, we chucked the non-original door speaker out of our Honda CRX and made a reducer plate to get an Infinity 5.25in coaxial in there. This just squeaks in on the depth front, but with the new baffle and some sound deadening, it sounds peachy.

01 We removed the Honda's speaker mounting ring when we took the door apart to do the sound deadening. This is going to be the template for the Infinity's spacer ring. It's being cut from 15mm MDF sheet to give the required magnet clearance. One little tip here is to cut the speaker hole before you cut the ring out from the MDF sheet. It's much more manageable then.

02 Once we've cut out the speaker hole and the spacer, we mark and drill the screw holes. This funky drill bit lets you drill a pilot hole and then countersink a bigger hole just by pushing it further into the wood. The countersink lets us re-use the original Honda screws.

03 We mark up the speaker screw holes so we can point the tweeters roughly in the right direction. We don't have to be exact at this point because they're fitted on swivel mounts and can be aimed where we want them once they're in the door.

The door panel is back in place over the new construction. We've left it unpainted for this picture because it's easier to see what we've done. Now you can also see that the tweeter is aiming slightly up and back into the car, which is about right. If it needs adjusting, we only have to take the door grille off to get to it. And that's it – job done.

Here's the ancient speaker that we removed from the car before we started the sound deadening. As you can tell by the rust, it looks as though a bit of damp has got to it, so we put a shield over the top of the new speaker to keep the water off.

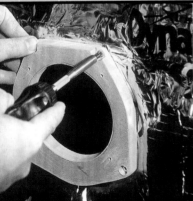

04 The ring goes on to the Dynamatted door. Simple, really.

06

07

05 And this is the Infinity being screwed in place. Notice we're using a hand screwdriver rather than a powered one. When you are tightening a screw into MDF you can get a better feel for how tight the screw's going before it strips itself free.

Achtung! *MDF dust is nasty stuff to breathe in. Wear a mask when you're cutting, drilling or sanding it.*

When there's no alternative to making a new speaker mounting, you might as well do a proper job. We designed this door build to hold a couple of six-in mids and a single tweeter. It's the sort of thing you'd do if you wanted lots of output to keep up with a barrage of subs sitting behind you, rather than just have all that bass drown the front out.

Door build -
twin sixes

That isn't where it normally goes

01 We begin by getting a feel for the shape of the build by looking at the fully assembled panel and seeing where we can start our new construction.

Fitting two mids in each door means buying two sets of components, but you could always just buy one set, make the speaker builds to accept the twinned drivers, and then just add the second pair when you could afford them. The extra tweeter that would come with the additional component set could be fitted on the mirror panel or A-pillar to help lift and widen the sound stage in the car, so nothing would go to waste.

Our door panel has a long pocket that needs integrating into the build's design. The pocket means we can integrate the two bits together to make it look something like a funky factory option rather than an obviously added-on lump. The panel actually came from a Toyota, but apart from the shape of the bits attached to it, it doesn't differ much from most other door trims, so you can adapt this technique to almost any car.

MDF sandwich

For this job we used three layers of MDF, sandwiched together with glass fibre reinforced paste. We did this because we've used the cloth-and-resin method in another project and we didn't want to show it twice. We're also assuming that you probably don't have easy access to something specialised like a router. This way, anyone with a jigsaw can have a go.

108

02 We strip the pocket from the door by unscrewing it from the back of the panel, keeping the screws to one side for reassembly later.

03 With the pocket stripped off, it seems logical to go forward from the centre pocket brace. The panel is unobstructed enough to allow the twin-driver build.

04 We make a cardboard template of the basic outline we want. We know roughly what speaker layout we're going to use, so the base has to be big enough to accommodate the mounting baffle and still look in balance with the rest of the pocket.

By using the two grille rings and the tweeter mounting pod from the JBL speakers we're fitting in this section, we can draw out where everything goes. **05**

Having the basic shape to work with, the speaker arrangement can be worked out. We make the baffle big enough so that the grille would push into the lip, but go around the chassis of the speakers. **06**

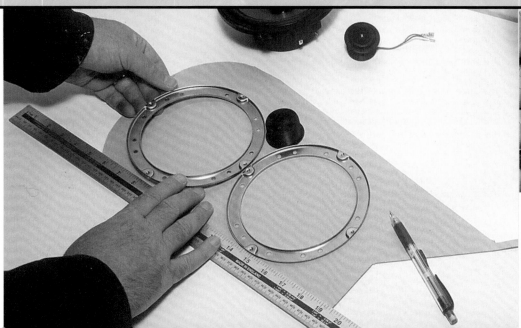
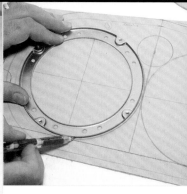

The template is cut very carefully into three pieces to give us the three layers of the door build. We use the outside of the template to give us the base board shape. Once this is cut out of the 9mm MDF sheet, we trim the template to the size of the speaker mounting baffle, and draw and cut that as well. The final stage is cutting the baffle surround shape from the template, and replicating it in MDF. Then we have the three layers we need.

07

This is the MDF jigsaw puzzle we're left with. The base piece and the mounting baffle are 9mm sheet, but the top piece is 12mm thick. This will give enough room for the grille to be pushed into without it interfering with the speaker cones when they're thrashing back and forth.

08

To assemble the skeleton of the build, we use a few 30mm-wide spacers cut from scrap MDF. These are hot-glued in place to support the baffle on top of the base board. The grille-surround ring is wood-glued and brad nailed in place so that it's extremely strong. We don't want this to separate from the baffle.

09

14 Once you're happy with the first application of filler, spend a bit longer getting it as smooth as possible. This will save time and effort later when you're rubbing it down.

Once the initial application has hardened, we take the 40-grit production paper to it. You can also use a small Surform for removing the first lot of rough stuff. If you hit the filler just before it's finally cured, it comes off really easily and the Surform doesn't clog up like the production paper.

15 A small offcut of wood is used as a joining block. This is screwed to the back end of the build, and the pocket is screwed into it. This joint will take all the strain between the two pieces, leaving the filler to bridge the gap smoothly without any undue stress.

16 The area of the door panel underneath the joint is masked up to stop any filler getting stuck to the panel when the two pieces are joined in-situ. Then the build and pocket are reattached. This is the best way to join the pieces because they are aligned exactly as they'll be when they go back into the car.

More hairy filler is smeared across the joint, with a bit more attention paid to the final curvy look required for the transition from pocket to build. Plenty of filler is rammed into the joint to give it support, even though the screwed block is taking most of the weight.

10 While the glue is drying, we chop up the original pockets, losing everything in front of the centre support. We know where the new bit comes up to, and any fine trimming can be done when we're joining the two pieces together.

11 Here's the finished jigsaw puzzle, ready for filling up.

12 Now we have to fill the gap between the baffle and base boards, which means rubber gloves and glass fibre filler. This bridging compound is strong but not too heavy, and it sands down nicely to give a reasonable finish. We use offcuts of steel mesh to give some support to the filler while it hardens, as well as using some gaffa tape on easier-to-reach sections. If you can't find anything suitable, you can always use the aluminium mesh sold for car body repairs.

13 The first blobs of filler are mixed up and applied to the space between the top and bottom plates. Consult the instructions on the tin for the exact ratio of filler to hardener, but once you've mixed it a couple of times, you'll get a feel for how long to mix it, how long it stays usable and when it's ready to sand down. The main thing is to get the filler applied quickly, work it into the mesh properly and get all the air bubbles out of it.

17 The filler is left for about an hour to set really solid before we disturb it by removing the build from the door panel. The joint is rock solid, so we set to with more 40-grit paper. Wearing gloves helps you to avoid rubbing through your finger ends, and you can still tell by feel when a bit is rough or smooth. Feeling if the panel is smooth enough is much better than trying to check it by eye.

18 As you rub down thick filler, you're bound to find some air bubbles under the surface. Pop them with a knife so that you can fill them in with smooth filler and make the surface good enough to trim.

19 After the smooth filler has been applied, the biggest lumps are removed with the Surform again, and then it's back to the 40-grit paper. After a few minutes' sanding, which includes a bit of help from an electric sander as well as the block, the panel is finally the right shape. The final sanding is done with 220-grit wet and dry paper. Then it's almost ready for vinyling.

20 Before trimming the panel, we spray the speaker baffle black. This is better than leaving it bare-MDF colour, which doesn't look good when you take the grille off. Once the paint has dried, we mask it off so we can spray glue on to the panel without messing up the painted bit.

21 We're trimming this build with black vinyl, so it has to be really smooth to stop the imperfections showing through. Of all the trim materials, vinyl has to be the most unforgiving – it's smooth and reflective, so any ripples under the surface really stand out.

We start by spraying a small area in the centre of the panel with glue, and the corresponding part of the vinyl trim. We cut this about three or four inches bigger all round than it needs to be to give some room for manoeuvre. We also heat the vinyl a little before we start the process, and then use a hot air gun to get the vinyl really soft when we really need to stretch. Be very careful not to overheat the vinyl and damage it, or your fingers.

Once the glue has gone tacky, we carefully put the vinyl on to the panel. By gluing only a small section at a time, we don't get any problems with the vinyl sticking in the wrong area. This also allows us to make sure we've got all the creases out before we stick the next bit.

22 Moving slowly across the panel, we glue and stick a few inches at a time until we have the back end finished. The vinyl needs a bit of pulling into shape to stop it puckering around the lower curve, but a quick blast with the heat gun sorts that.

23 The front of the build is a bit more difficult, but again, with a bit of heat in the right place, the wrinkles can be pulled out and the surface left smooth.

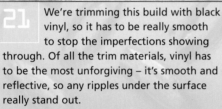

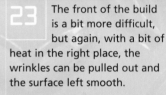

Once the speakers have been fitted, we can get on with the grille. It's made from 6mm MDF, cut to the same shape as the piece we've removed from the top slice of the door build. With a bit of light sanding, it's a snug fit in the trimmed build.

28

The grille cloth is stretched out ready for gluing and sticking to the trim ring.

29

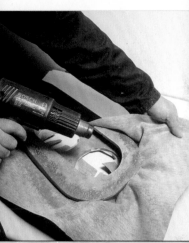

24 The heat gun is very useful for softening the vinyl enough to get it to lie flat around the tighter corners. Once the creases have been pulled on to the back of the panel, we glue and staple the vinyl flat.

25 After the first lot of staples, we trim all the lumps and bumps off the vinyl so that the build sits nice and flat on the door panel.

26 In some places, a couple of staples are needed to make sure the vinyl doesn't move about.

27 The vinyl around the speaker aperture is stuck in the same way as the back. Where there is a little tension, we've added a couple of staples to hold it in place, but most of the way round the lip, the vinyl sticks very strongly. Then we fit it to the door and drop the drivers into position to see what it looks like. Notice how the mids have been twisted round slightly so that there's room for the tweeter mounting. This allows us to get the three drivers into the smallest footprint possible.

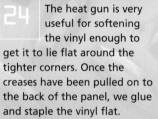

Then the ring and fabric are glued before they're pulled together. For a neat finish, take great care to cover as little of the grille cloth with glue as you can. We used the

30 template as a mask to prevent glue overspray.

We pull one side at a time on to the trim ring, getting the wrinkles out as we go. A few staples are needed to be on the safe side, but most

31 of the fabric holds on with the glue.

With the grille in place, you can see the finished build in position. Note that we've used slightly contrasting colours of vinyl and grille cloth. This is purely to let you see more easily in the

32 photograph what we've done.

Glass fibre
kickpanels

Sometimes it's almost impossible to get the right shaped enclosures using wood – for instance, an interesting shaped box fitted into a curved area. But fabricating a couple of speaker enclosures out of glass fibre can be a great way to do it. Practise the technique on your kickpanels and then you'll be ready to tackle something larger, such as building a moulded bass cabinet.

The idea of sticking speakers way down in the kickpanels may seem a bit strange. Why put speakers that low when you want the sound to arrive from somewhere outside the windscreen? Well, in some cars, these types of builds produce just such an effect.

One of the main reasons that kickpanel enclosures are popular is because they help with path-length equalisation. That's a long-winded way of saying both front speaker sets are about the same distance away from the listening position, and because of that, neither side dominates the sound. So the sound stage is spread much more evenly across the car, and if you're trying to get a realistic live-band effect, you'll be a lot closer to it.

These enclosures can work exceptionally well in some cars, but they're also completely useless in others. While there aren't any definitive laws on which cars work and which don't, there are a few pointers.

If your car is very short and you sit very upright, they probably won't work that well. If it's long and you feel quite low in the vehicle, they could perform effectively. But if you've got a large transmission tunnel and a big centre console, they might struggle again. If you've got a wide car with hardly any tunnel between the seats and no console at all, you really want to give them a try.

If you've got a left-hand-drive automatic with loads of room in the kickwells, get your woofers in there, too. There's loads of room in these cars because there's no clutch pedal, and th other two pedals are near the tunnel.

01 The first job is to cut the baffle for the Focal component set we've chosen for this install. The grille and tweeter mounting are positioned where we want them, and then drawn round to give us the classic teardrop baffle.

02 The two circles are joined up and the template is cut from the card sheet.

03 This gives a good idea of what we're trying to achieve with the finished item.

04 This is roughly the final position of the baffle, but it will be different when we've finished. Obviously, we're showing the passenger-side panel being made, but you should do your initial design on the driver's side, taking into account the pedal position so you don't compromise your heel-and-toe technique when you're driving.

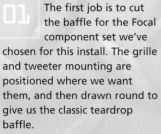

The footwell needs masking up to protect it from the polyester resin that will applied to the glass fibre. Two layers of tape are stuck to the carpet, and we work up the bulkhead, overlapping the tape with the open edge at the low side so that any resin will run down the tape rather than into it.

05

This small side trim is cut from the one-piece sill moulding because it is too unwieldy as a single piece. This little trim will be moulded into the new build, so it will look like Honda did it.

06

With the baffle still part of the main MDF sheet, the tweeter position is cut out with a hole saw. These things are great when the hole is too small for a jigsaw. The hole saw is about the same diameter as the tweeter pod, so once the hole is drilled, a quick sanding allows the mounting cup to fit perfectly.

07

The mid-range-driver hole is chopped out with a jigsaw, keeping slightly to the inside of the drawn line to make the speaker a snug fit in the baffle.

08

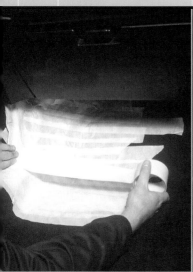

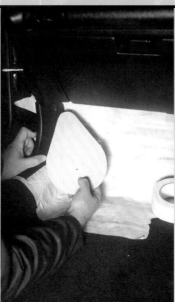

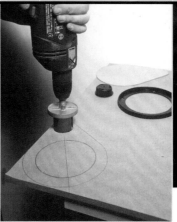

09 Before we cut the baffle from the MDF sheet we try both speakers in their new home, and they both like it. Now's the time to get messy.

10 The glass-fibre mat needs to be cut into shape. Then a slit allows it to bend in the footwell and follow the contour of the carpet.

11 To aid the release of the glass fibre panel, the masking tape is coated with a thin layer of wax polish. This stuff stops the resin from taking hold, making for a clean break when the panel needs to be removed.

12 With everything ready to start – matting cut, tape polished, and brush and roller ready – the resin and catalyst are weighed and mixed. Between 2-3 per cent by weight of hardener is added to the resin before a thorough mixing with an old screwdriver. For 500g of resin, we use 12g of hardener.

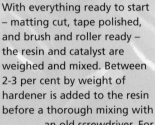

17 The masking tape pulls off the back of the panel easily thanks to the wax polish.

18 Once the panel has been cut down to remove the hairy bits of un-resined matting, the support wedge is screwed in place and the baffle is joined to it to check that everything still looks okay.

19 The overall shape of the build is arrived at by loosely drawing round the baffle to get a rounded outline. Then it's cut out with a jigsaw. Be especially careful not to breathe in the glass dust at this point.

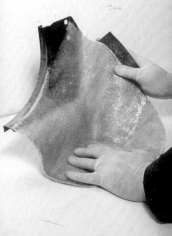

20 The edges of the back panel are sanded smooth to stop any injury, and to make it easy to join the front material to it.

13 A cheap paintbrush is the best tool for getting started with the resin application. Slap plenty of resin on to and into the matting, stippling the brush against the fibres to get the mat totally soaked through. Once the first layer is sodden, the second piece of matting can be applied and more resin stippled in.

14 To get maximum saturation of resin into mat, a roller is the best tool. This pushes trapped air out of the matting and makes for a very even take-up of resin throughout the piece.

15 Once the resin has gone off completely, a small wedge of MDF is cut out to support the baffle during the next stages. The baffle is checked for alignment until the wedge is the right shape and size, and then the new panel can be removed.

16 Because the masking tape has only a gentle grip on the floor, the build pulls out easily. Make sure you are dealing with a completely cured piece of glass fibre before you disturb it from its mould. The piece can warp and alter as it cures, so it isn't unusual to find that something which fitted perfectly a day or two ago doesn't fit properly after it has finally cured.

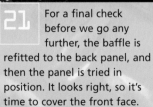

21 For a final check before we go any further, the baffle is refitted to the back panel, and then the panel is tried in position. It looks right, so it's time to cover the front face.

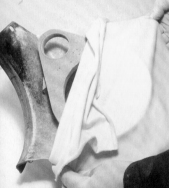

22 Fleecy material is stretched over the baffle and round the edges to give this flowing shape. It attaches using hot glue on the rear side of the back panel.

23 Once all the wrinkles are stretched out of the fleece, resin is plastered on to it. A 300g batch proves to be just about right with hardly any wastage.

24 After waiting for this part to dry, excess material is trimmed from the edges and the mid-mounting hole is cut out to make the enclosure easier to handle.

25 When the build feels like it has fully cured and is completely solid, the surface is rubbed down to make it smooth-ish. Then we give it a quick splash of filler to finish it off.

26 More waiting, and a lot of rubbing down follows. The enclosure is now ready for its first proper test-fit.

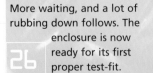

27 Then the enclosure is lined up and drilled along with the inner footwell panel. This is for the fitting screw that will stop it falling out during spirited driving.

28 To deaden the enclosure, we use Focal's *Plain Chant* deadening foam sheets. The sheets need to be cut down to go in, but once they're stuck to the sides of the box they make quite a difference.

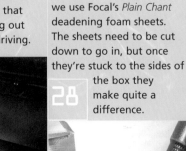

29 The next step is the fiddly gluing and covering. Like all our previous trimmed builds, small areas of glue are sprayed at a time, to allow the vinyl to be heated up and then stretched into place.

30 This is the flip-side of the build, showing the overlapped vinyl being glued to the edges of the enclosure.

31 Once the speaker holes are cut out, the box is drilled for speaker wires and filled with enclosure wadding. This is necessary, even on smaller drivers, to damp any unwanted noises from the box.

32 The finished build looks a good match for the other black furnishings around it, and the speakers look pretty cool, too. Now all that's needed is a custom floor mat to fit around the build.

Tweeter builds

01 We use the tweeter mounting-cup from the JL Audio VR-075 tweeter set to give us an idea of the shape we'd like to incorporate into the trim piece.

There are a few guidelines about tweeter placement. For the best results, the tweeter and mid range should be as close together as possible – generally. Yes, there's that word again. Generally means just that, and in some cases, having a tweeter right next to the mid range won't work that well because the acoustics of the vehicle won't allow it to.

So what do you do in a case like that? Once you've got your mids mounted and you are happy with what they are doing, you should try alternative mounting points for the tweeters to find out where they work best. The easiest way is to connect them up on long lengths of speaker wire and Blu-tack them in various places until you find out where they seem to do the best job. Then all you have to do is build some form of location for them.

The A-pillar trim is a popular position that works well on a lot of cars. Then you just play around with their firing angle so that you get the results you want. Most tweeter sets come with two or three mounting options in the kit, so you have some choice over how you can install them, but to give a nice factory-fitted look, you can do better. Here's what we came up with for a trim piece that wouldn't have accepted a surface or flush-mount tweeter.

02 Having cut out a nice oval shape in cardboard, we transfer that to some 6mm MDF sheet and draw an inner line to give us the grille insert size. We'll cut the grille from Foamex sheet, mainly because it's dead easy to cut with a knife and you can sand it quickly to get a perfect fit. You can use MDF or plywood if you can't find Foamex.

03 The oval is chopped out and ready to go. We've sanded it lightly to clean it up, so now we can work out where it's going on the pillar trim, and mark which bit of the plastic needs to be removed.

>

04 The easiest way to remove the excess plastic from the trim is to cut it out with a Dremel tool, fitted with a cutting disc. This tool is ideal for making small cuts in lightweight material, where something like a jigsaw would be too cumbersome.

05 With the hole roughly cut out, we hot-glue the MDF ring into position before adding the glass fibre filler.

06 We scratch the plastic trim panel heavily with a knife, which helps the filler to key on to the surface. This means that when we start sanding it, we won't get the filler falling off in lumps.

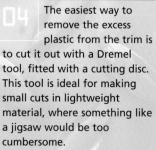

When the whole panel is trimmed, the material covering the speaker hole is slit open and worked into the opening to give a smoothly trimmed aperture. The excess material behind the panel is carefully cut off using a sharp scalpel. 'Carefully' means minding not to cut through panel or skin.

A piece of Alcantara is chopped out to be a bit bigger than the trim piece. We spray both the material and the panel with contact adhesive, then let the glue go tacky before we start joining the two together.

11 We start at the bottom end of the trim, working the material into place carefully to keep creases and wrinkles at bay. If you're unsure about the trimming, you can always spray a few inches at a time, work it into place and then glue some more.

12 Those scalpel blades are very sharp when they're new.

13 This is the Foamex grille. It's been cut to size, allowing a little room all round it for the speaker cloth that will cover it. Then it's drilled and opened out with a cone drill bit so that some sound will get out.

14

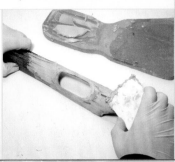

07 The filler takes up the shape between the ring and the trim, and we take the time to do as much smoothing as possible, so that we have the least rubbing down to do once it's gone off. To support the filler across the hole between the trim and the back of the ring, we've just used a bit of gaffa tape.

08 Now we can knock down the rough fibre filler before moving on to the smooth paste. It's important to get the basic shape in at this stage, otherwise you'll be sanding away all the smooth stuff as well as the rough filler underneath later.

09 After the rough comes the smooth. With the heavy filler rubbed down, we move on to the smooth stuff to fill in the pits and holes left in the surface of the build. We also repair the area of the MDF ring damaged by a slip with a round file while chomping out the filler. Accidents happen to us all.

10 After more rubbing down with very fine paper, the build is really taking shape. The very tiniest of pinholes won't trouble us because the whole trim will be covered in Alcantara, which is expensive suede lookalike. If you were spraying the trim with paint for a shiny finish, you'd need more filler and more rubbing. Notice that the whole trim has been roughly sanded to give a keyed surface for the trim glue.

Through the hole you can see a rounded-out bit, which will accept the tweeter when the part is fitted into the car. Because we have done away with the mounting bracket, the tweeter will be held in place with a dab of hot glue. This works fine holding something small and light like a tweeter, and the speaker can be removed and the glue scraped off if necessary.

With the grille cloth face-side down, a piece of masking tape is cut out exactly the same size as the grille. This is stuck to the cloth, which is then sprayed with glue. The back of the grille is also glued. When the glue has gone off enough, the masking tape is removed, and the grille is placed on the dry bit. Then we just pull **15** the sticky cloth on to the sticky grille.

After stretching the cloth round the grille, the excess material is scalpeled off as **16** neatly as possible to leave the finished grille insert.

And that's it. Dead easy. The only thing left now is to put it back into the car and play around with the **17** tweeter angling before gluing it in place.

Believe it or not, there are people who don't like bass. There are even so-called music fans who screw up their faces and whine about that unnecessary thumping when the wick gets turned up. Well, if that's you, you might want to skip on to the next chapter, where we talk about cool things like installing amps and equalisers and stuff. But if you're a thumper, keep reading.

Before we talk about getting rumble into your car, it might surprise you know just how much bass there is in different types of music, especially if you

12 Bass camp

have very club-orientated tastes. Even though you may reckon nothing can beat the thud from a banging house tune, you'll probably find a lot mo low-end info in something classical. Seriously.

Anything played on a large pipe organ will have notes that drop through the floor. To replay them, you need plenty of cone area and a fair bit of power to drive it. And there are quite a few modern synthesised performances of classical pieces like Bach's Toccata and Fugue that hit so hard it's difficult to believe they were written so long ago. If you like a bit of thump, try something like that on your system. You might get a shock at how good it sounds.

Anyway, now the bass-lite posse has gone, let's talk about sub-bass and how to get it in a car. We're going to be looking at realistic amounts of bass rather than the SPL contest-winning amounts used in competition cars. It still means plenty of grunt, but not to the point where you'll need heavy duty suspension to cope with the weight of gear, or ear plugs to turn out system up all the way.

Although bass is as important to the music as any other range, it's difficult to get good bass reproduction in a car for various reasons. The main one is because outside noises can drown out or muddy the lower frequencies we want to hear. Road noise, engine noise, exhaust roar and the like all contribute to cancelling out the bass notes. This means we have to do something a bit more than fit some slightly bigger speakers.

A lot of domestic hi-fi nuts used to sneer at car stereo enthusiasts and say there was no need for all that power and huge sub woofers to get real bass performance. Well, for one thing their precious listening rooms never had engines and wheels and noisy tyres, and they never drove them at 70mph down the motorway, so they didn't have the bass-swamping background noise to get over.

For another, domestic hi-fi companies are now selling sub woofers as fast as they can make them. That's because home cinema systems need the throbability of a sub to get the real impact of a film across, and hi-fi freaks are finally realising what they've been missing for years. So we've got the last laugh.

Sealed bass enclosure

The simplest bass box design is the sealed enclosure. But just because it's a simple design, that doesn't mean you can chuck one together and expect to get the best performance from your sub.

To show you how to make a decent sealed enclosure, we took a dinky little 15in sub woofer, built a box for it and fitted it into the Vectra SRi you'll see in the chapter on amps. And speaking of fitting, you must always screw a sub box down or it could be a real liability in an accident. Sure, *you* aren't going to have an accident, but someone else might hit you and the result would be the same. A hefty sub box tearing through the car will wreak untold havoc – on you and your car. So bolt the sucker in properly.

We used a JL Audio 15W6, which needs a cabinet volume of just 1.25 cubic feet – plus 0.135 cubic feet for its own displacement and any extra volume for bracing. This means you don't have to lose all your boot space to run something pretty big that can go very loud and hit very hard.

In fact, this thing can hit *very* hard, as well as being capable of playing really intricate bass lines. But it will only do the job properly when it's fitted into the correct-size box, so here's how we went on.

We worked out that the external dimensions of our box were going to be 17.5in x 17.5in x 11in, giving the required 2443-cubic inch internal volume. This figure came from the following little sum. Our woofer needs 1.25 cubic feet of airspace, it needs 0.135 cubic feet to cover its own displacement, and we wanted 50 cubic inches to account for the very necessary brace. Add the first two figures together to get 1.385 cubic feet, then multiply by 1728 – the number of cubic inches in a cubic foot. That gives a grand total of 2443 cubic inches as our required internal volume. Because we are building the box from 0.75in MDF, the internal dimensions are 1.5in shorter in each direction, so that gives us 16in x 16in x 9.5in. Still with us?

To get a deadly accurate set of cuts, we bought the MDF from our local DIY store and had them chop it on their massive power saw. All we had to do was plan how we wanted the sheet cut up and they did the rest. We paid a little more for the privilege, but ended up with a flat-pack sub box sliced perfectly to our design. If you can't cut a perfect straight edge with a jigsaw – and who can? – this saves a load of heartache.

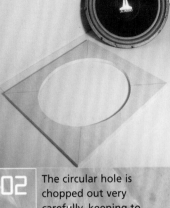
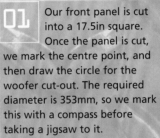

01 Our front panel is cut into a 17.5in square. Once the panel is cut, we mark the centre point, and then draw the circle for the woofer cut-out. The required diameter is 353mm, so we mark this with a compass before taking a jigsaw to it.

02 The circular hole is chopped out very carefully, keeping to the line as closely as possible. This way we'll get the maximum seal between the lip of the woofer and the edge of the baffle. In fact, we have to gently file a couple of high spots off the baffle to get the sub to seat snugly in place. Notice that the baffle is quite a bit bigger than the woofer, allowing for a very strong edge that will be able to support the speaker properly without crumbling under the strain. And there will be a lot of strain.

03 Once the screw holes have been marked and drilled out, T-nuts are hammered into the baffle from behind. A T-nut has four sharp prongs that grip into the MDF baffle as it is put into place, and the M5 thread takes a cap-headed Allen bolt. A full set of eight of these bolts and nuts does a great job of holding the speaker solidly and preventing any air leaks around the driver lip.

This one might seem odd, but for a bit of extra strength we glass-fibre the T-nuts into position. This does two things. Firstly, it seals the T-nut up completely, so there's no way we can get an air leak past one of them should a bolt work loose. Secondly, the glass paste stops the T-nut falling out of the baffle if the sub is ever removed.

04

We've inserted a bolt into each nut to stop any glass fibre goo from getting into the threads. By waiting until the paste has *almost* set, we can remove the bolt without it getting stuck in place either.

05

Once the baffle is finished, we start to assemble the cabinet. We put it together using PVA wood glue and 2in woodscrews. This really is a bit of belt and braces, because the glue is strong enough to hold the box together on its own. By using a couple of screws on each joint, it just means we can handle the box while the glue is still drying. The only panel we haven't fitted at this stage is the back one and you'll see why in the next shot.

06

10

To get the woofer to line up permanently with the Vectra's drop-down rear armrest, we fix it solidly in place using steel brackets. Two brackets are bolted into the strong box section at the front of the back shelf. The enclosure is screwed to these using good strong woodscrews so that it won't work its way loose over time.

11

The front of the box is fastened to a custom steel bracket made to fit on to a rear-seat mounting-point. This way, the box is supported correctly and won't become a threat if the car is ever involved in an accident. You can't see it from this position, but the enclosure is sitting on a piece of MDF that runs the full width of the box, so it isn't just hanging from the shelf brackets. Happy that it fits properly, all we need to do is remove it, fill it with wadding and trim it up.

12

We start trimming the box by getting a big piece of carpet and cutting it roughly to size. Then we spray glue on to the face of the box, being careful not to get any on the wadding, which had been added. The corresponding area of carpet is glued, and once it has gone tacky, the face of the box is wrapped.

07 There are two jobs to do before we fit the back panel to the box. The first is to fill all the joins with more glass fibre filler paste. This gives a bit more strength as well as making sure the thing is absolutely airtight. This is a fiddly job, but a bit of determination gets it smeared all round the joints before it goes off.

08 The other job is to fit the bracing piece. This helps to pull the top and bottom panels together, and stops the back panel from flexing like a very thick drum skin. We attach it using screws into all three joints and then lump a bit of filler on to it as well.

09 Once the back panel is fitted, more glass fibre paste is splodged around the back edges to complete the sealing operation. Here you can see the brace stuck in position through the woofer opening. You can also see why we cut the piece out of the brace to clear the magnet assembly.

Where the excess carpet has been folded up, we flatten it down neatly. Then we cut a straight line through the fold using a steel ruler and a craft knife with a new blade. Once the excess is removed, the carpet butts up perfectly and you can't see the joints. **13**

Drill a hole for the speaker wire and feed it through. (You should eventually seal the hole for best results). The woofer wiring is soldered in place before dropping the sub back into the box. When you do something like this, make sure you have enough spare wire in the box so you can do it without struggling. **14**

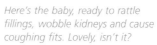

Here's the baby, ready to rattle fillings, wobble kidneys and cause coughing fits. Lovely, isn't it?

Here's a quick question: what do you keep in your glovebox? Tapes? Sweets? Cigarettes? Well, how about putting some bass in there? If you have the right kind of glovebox, it's an easy job, and so long as you don't expect brain-crushing bass, it's a worthwhile one, too. The idea is to get up-front bass so that all the music appears to be coming from somewhere along your bonnet rather than having most of the band at the front and the bass in the back.

Glovebox
bass box

Bass camp

A lot of gloveboxes are big enough to make into speaker cabinets now that we have small bass speakers that don't need large boxes. The Focal 5WS subs are only as big as a standard 125mm speaker but they are a true sub woofer, so fitting them in the dash should help to pull the bass well forward in the car.

01

06 The next job is to sound deaden the three plastic walls that aren't going to be covered in MDF. We're using Dynamat Xtreme because it sticks really well without using a heatgun, and it's very thin so it doesn't take up any of the airspace in the box. We know the enclosure is a bit tight for a pair of 5WS subs, so we don't want to lose any more with thick deadening material.

07 It's vital to get a good bond between the Dynamat and the glovebox, so we roller it until it is absolutely solid.

08 Next we mix a blob of glass fibre filler that's going to be used to stick the lid and baffle on to the glovebox, and seal all the holes in the enclosure. By smearing the filler around the speaker holes, we effectively seal the baffle on to the 'box. This piece is screwed to the top plate, which is also screwed into the box at each side. When all the screws are tightened, the filler squeezes out between the wood and plastic, so we squeeze it back into all the cracks we can see and leave it to set.

The glovebox needs two new panels – one to block it off on the top and one on the back for a mounting baffle. A card template is made for the top plate because it's a more awkward shape to get right.

02

Then the plate is cut from 18mm MDF. We're using MDF this thick to give plenty of strength and make the small box as acoustically dead as possible. The top plate needs a lot of shaping to get it to fit into the tapered sides of the box.

03

The speaker baffle is dead easy to cut once we've measured the panel. Then we cut out the speaker mounting holes and fit the baffle to the glovebox. Cutting the holes in the glovebox calls for a bit of care to prevent the plastic from cracking when it is being jigsawed.

04

The speakers are test-fitted – now is not a good time to find out that they're too deep to go in – and the screw positions marked for drilling.

05

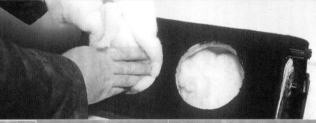

11 Before the speakers are fitted, the box is filled with wadding. This helps to damp the cabinet and also fools the speakers into behaving as though they are fitted into a slightly larger box. It's a very worthwhile thing to do to any speaker enclosure, and particularly a sub-bass one.

Then all we have to do is screw the woofers into place. Now isn't that better than a packet of fags and some old parking tickets? And with the glovebox lid closed, you'd never know they were there.

12

09 Because this will be a hidden cabinet, we plan on trimming it in carpet, which is very forgiving of what's underneath it. This means we can give the box just a quick sand to get rid of the hairiest bits of filler that stick out from the edges. Then we can spray the box with glue, before wrapping it with carpet.

10 A piece of carpet is chopped to be about 4 in bigger than the area we want to trim. As usual, we glue a small section of carpet and box, before bringing them together and smoothing out the creases. We start at the top of the box, being careful not to spray any glue into the lock mechanism. Once the carpet is really stuck in place, we cut out the speaker holes.

Rack 'em up

You'll need to find somewhere for your amps and processors if your a vehicle has only ever had standard gear fitted. You may get away with using the original locations for the head unit and speakers, but everything else will mean new construction. The ideas and techniques we'll show here can be used for any bulky electronic doobries, so pick the one that suits your needs the best.

Most cars have a few places where amps can be fitted. However, there are plenty of things to consider when choosing where to install your gear. And just because we suggest somewhere as suitable for an amp rack, that doesn't mean it's going to be right for everyone. You also need to decide whether you're going to fit your amp as stealthily as you can or make a real show of it.

Amp racks can be made in a few different ways, depending on how low key or showy it has to be, and where it's going to be fitted. The simplest method is to get a piece of MDF or plywood – a little bigger than the equipment that's being fitted to it – and just screw it into the car somewhere out of the way. But amp racks can get a lot more involved than a bit of a plank and that's when they get to be more fun.

The boot is the most obvious place to stick an amp rack, but this area causes the most problems with the first question. Normally, there will be somewhere to mount a board securely to some steelwork and the amp can be screwed to that. In a lot of cars, you might have to make up some brackets to hold the board, but you should be able to get everything nice and solid without having to drill through to the outside of the car.

For some people, a mounting board on the boot floor isn't an option, especially if their motor carts around heavy gear. There's always the option of a covered rack to protect the amp from anything lobbed into the luggage area, but then there's the cooling issue, which we'll come to in a moment.

There are lots of other options, though, such as under the boot floor, behind rear side panels and on the floor of the passenger

There are several things to consider when choosing a place for an amp rack. The main ones are fairly easy to spot.

1. **Will the amp/processor get in the way of valuable space?**

2. **Will the unit receive sufficient cooling air in its new home?**

3. **Is there any chance it will get wet?**

4. **Is the new supporting panel strong enough to stop the gear going walkies if you have a shunt?**

5. **Will it get damaged by feet or luggage?**

All these questions need considering before you bash on and get building.

compartment. These all use up space that isn't normally needed for anything else, but they do require a bit of thought over to the second and third questions.

If you're thinking of fitting an amplifier into an enclosed space – and that includes a covered rack – you should consider how to help the amp's cooling system. An amp gets warm just by doing its job, and if you put it into sealed area, it could get hot enough to shut down or do itself some damage. Normally an amp turns itself off if it gets too warm, but running one hot enough to 'thermal' will still stress it out quite a bit. However, there are ways to help an amp keep cool, and they needn't cost a fortune.

Plenty of manufacturers that supply installation hardware have varying sizes of fans available, and you can also find them in electronics shops that sell gear for building computers. Fans come in a couple of designs. There's the round cooling fan, which you fit over a hole so that it sucks air in or blows it out of the sealed area, or there's a linear fan.

Linear fans look like a long thin waterwheel and they do a great job of blowing air across a wide area. They're particularly useful when lined up with an amp's heatsink because they can blow air right down the cooling fins. They're more expensive than rotary fans, though, so check which method is going to cool your amp more efficiently and then check your wallet.

Adding a fan to the rack isn't the end of the cooling story. There's no point in simply circulating the warm air round and around the rack. You need some way of getting cool air into the system.

If you're building your system in the boot of your car, have a look behind the trim panels for the car's stale-air vents. These are often hidden behind the bumper moulding and they usually have something like a rubber flap to stop any water from being blown back into the boot.

If the vent is there, you can hook a piece of flexy pipe up to it. Run the pipe out of sight under the boot floor and behind the trim panels, then join it to the fan intake to allow fresh air to blow straight into the rack. Some cars have the vents on the B-pillar under the door lock catch, so you have to run the pipe into the car. Even so, it's generally not a bad job to do. Either way, cool air gives your amp an easier life.

To put your amp right out of the way behind a rear quarter panel, you won't need to worry as much about the rack. Most amps can be hung from brackets that attach to the steelwork around the rear-quarter area. And if there are some vents that breathe straight into the airspace, you've solved the cooling problem, too. Bargain. There's one final thing to bear in mind. If you need to get to your amp, to tweak it or remove it for any reason, you'll to have to strip the side panel down. Sometimes it isn't the most convenient area to work in.

The other stealthy area to look at is on the floor, which usually means under a seat. This area seems tailor-made for amplifiers, but has more pitfalls than the other sites we've mentioned so far. The main one is water damage, which afflicts a surprising number of amps every year.

On older cars the floor is very often damp for a lot of the time. There are plenty of reasons for this, but the most common ones are failing door seals, badly fitted door speakers, faulty bulkhead grommets, blocked scuttle panel vents, blocked sunroof drain tubes and rust holes. If you want to have a go at siting your amps under your seats, check very carefully for any signs of water coming into the car before you commit to sticking them there.

If you find the reason for the leak and fix it, there's no reason why you can't stick an amp on the floor if there's room. But think

about your passengers and how heavy-footed they could be, not knowing your amp was under the seat in front of them. You'd be surprised what damage can be done if someone accidentally kicks or stands on an amplifier. In a small car without much room for legs and feet, that can happen all too often.

There's always in front of the front seat as another floor option. Unlike the rear footwell, which is trampled all over when someone gets into the car, the front footwell is mostly untouched. Many people get in the car by sitting down and then swinging their legs in, so the space directly in front of the seats is almost always foot-free.

As long as the item you fit there isn't too big, and as long as it's reasonably well protected from prying eyes and very well bolted down, there's no reason why you can't put things in front of both front seats. It works less well when the floor's very lumpy, though.

Side panel
amp rack

To show you a simple amp rack – but one with a couple of nice twists – we set about fitting a Genesis Profile Four into the boot of our Honda CRX VTEC SiR. The spaces behind the rear wheelarches looked ideal for hiding things away, and the Profile Four seemed a great fit in the driver's side cubby. All we had to do was figure out how to attach it to the car and then how to protect it from errant luggage.

01 Firstly, we check that the Genesis amp will fit into the chosen area. It falls in, so we have no worries about making the rack. And happily for us, there's a stale air vent behind the rack to draw warm air away from the amp's built-in fan cooling system. Result.

09 After spraying the rack satin black to tidy it up, it is fixed into place using a bracket made from the same strip bracket as the head unit rear support in Chapter 10. You can't see it too well because it's tucked away behind the rack, but it's held in place by a factory bolt. The bottom support sits in a hole in the floor that locates the Honda side panel. This way we end up with a rock-solid rack without drilling any new holes.

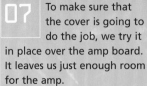

06 Using 9 mm MDF for the mounting board, we draw and cut the required shape from the template. With a little sanding, it's a nice neat fit, so then we figure out how to fix it in the car.

07 To make sure that the cover is going to do the job, we try it in place over the amp board. It leaves us just enough room for the amp.

08 To give us an idea of where the wires will enter the rack, we place the amp on the mounting board and draw where we want the holes for the cables.

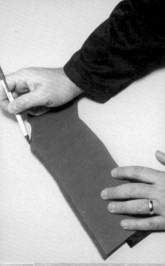

02 To get the right shape of template, we use a large profile gauge to give us the curvy contour of the boot liner. If you don't have a profile gauge, just mess about with the cardboard for longer. Think of it as an initiative test…

03 This shape is transferred on to a piece of card that's roughly the right size. It takes a few attempts, cutting and trying, but soon we have the shape of the board.

04 Test-fitting the template shows how far back the rack will sit into the recess, which means the amp will be well away from luggage and possible damage. It also shows the template's a good fit.

05 Out comes the profile gauge and cardboard again, as we make another panel to fit over the amplifier. This cover is going to be cut from 4 mm MDF because it doesn't need to support any weight, but it will protect the amp's stainless steel cover.

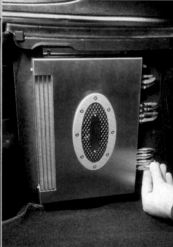

10 The amp is screwed in position once the wiring has been fed through the appropriate holes.

11 This is the finished amp, wired and ready to go. But what about that cover?

12 By pushing the MDF cover against the amp, the two rivets on the Genesis badge mark the back of the MDF. This gives us a cunning plan. We make an exact copy of the oval vent in cardboard, which we press against the amp to get the two rivet marks. After drawing round the shape and cutting it out, we have an oval hole in the cover that lines up over the amp's fan intake.

13 The finished item looks pretty good, with the fan intake on show and the amp protected from any damage. Note the little filler piece, which just makes the cover look that bit better finished off. It's 12 mm MDF, cut with the profile gauge and then glued into place. All in all, a straightforward job, but one that looks rather tidy.

Bigger rack

To do a more involved rack, we got hold of a few bits and pieces for installing into a Vauxhall Vectra SRi saloon. This is the one with the sub enclosure from the previous chapter, so it's only right we should be adding some amplification to drive the new sub and front speakers.

We designed the system around a gutsy Class D bass amp, and a powerful stereo amp for the front stage. The Directed amps aren't huge, so there was enough room for the KEF crossovers and the Directed 1.0 Farad capacitor. The amps have their own built-in crossovers, but the Alpine head unit also has a bass crossover and dedicated sub woofer output, so we used that to give us the sub signal.

The owner wanted a nice layout of equipment with a bit of shape and flow to it, but we had to make a hard-wearing cover for the new construction. The car is used for carting gear about in the boot, on either side of the sub box and on the back seat. After a consulting with the owner, we decided to trim things up in a dark grey carpet that matched the original boot panelling, just leaving a couple of windows for the amps. This is how we did it.

01 Here's the boot as Vauxhall intended. Our mission is to fill it with some kicking tunes, but leave as much room as possible. We also have to make sure the spare wheel is still accessible, along with the jack and wheelbrace.

02 The first thing to add to the boot is a rake of sound deadening. We stick several sheets of Dynamat Xtreme on to the boot floor and into the spare wheel well to quieten the back end down.

03 We also cover the rear shelf with Xtreme to stop any nasty buzzes and rattles once the bass gets cranked up. The sound-deadening sheet is applied with a hardwood wallpaper edge roller once the metalwork has been cleaned with some cellulose thinners on a rag. Applying the sheet to the underside of the shelf makes things nice and dead, so we don't need to do the top side.

04 We try to find an arrangement of the equipment that we all like, and that will be logical to wire. After playing with a few different ideas, we come up with this one. The amps look good on the slant, the crossovers are close to the front-speaker amp, and the power terminals of the bass amp are very close to the power cap terminals. We'll go for that, then.

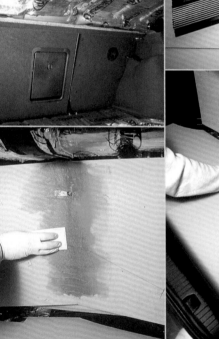
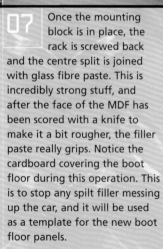

05 To make the rack sit vertically, a small block of wood is fixed to the bottom of the sub box. This will pack out the bottom of the rack and give it a firm base to be bolted to.

06 For a bit more visual interest, we decide to split the rack from top to bottom and put the two pieces on an angle. After we join the two bits together with steel strip and bend them to the required angle, we screw them to the back of the sub box.

07 Once the mounting block is in place, the rack is screwed back and the centre split is joined with glass fibre paste. This is incredibly strong stuff, and after the face of the MDF has been scored with a knife to make it a bit rougher, the filler paste really grips. Notice the cardboard covering the boot floor during this operation. This is to stop any spilt filler messing up the car, and it will be used as a template for the new boot floor panels.

08 The joint is covered up with another piece of MDF, which has been heavily sanded to blend into the angled rack. A couple of holes are cut into the top and bottom of the centre piece. This is to allow access to the mounting screws that hold the rack to the sub box, so we can remove the rack later on. Then we draw the shape of the new front edge of the floor on to the cardboard.

09 Having finished the card templates, we use to them to transfer the shapes on to pieces of thin plywood, which are going to be the new boot floor. After carefully cutting the plywood, we sand the edges smooth to lessen the chances of picking up a splinter.

10 To lift the floor high enough to clear the large spare wheel, battens are fixed to the underside of the plywood floor panels. This means that the boot will have a smooth, lump-free floor when we've finished.

11 The battens are just ordinary rough-sawn timber. There is no need to get the smooth-planed good stuff because it'll hardly ever be seen.

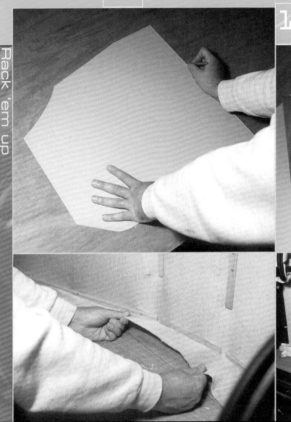

16 The fabric needs a bit of adjustment for it to lie without any wrinkles and keep an even tension across the areas not directly touching anything underneath. By unscrewing the wood strips, pulling the material a bit tighter and then refitting the strips, the whole sheet is nice and taut, ready for the resin.

17 The panel's almost ready to go. All we need to do now is refit the card floor templates to stop the new panels from being plastered in polyester resin.

18 After mixing up 500 grams of resin and hardener, we quickly apply it using a cheap paintbrush. The material changes colour when the resin soaks into it, so we just keep sloshing the resin about until the whole panel looks wetted through. Then we leave it for a few hours to set up before we remove it from the car.

12 The two pieces of floor fit like this. They are solid once they're in place, but they're also easy to get out should the spare wheel need to be accessed.

13 Now it's time to get messy – or rather, to prepare things for getting messy. Here the amps have been wrapped in clingfilm, then covered in masking tape. The small pieces of wood are being glued to the amp edges to give a bit of shape when the glass fibre resin starts flowing in a few minutes. Notice the blue-grey material at the top of the shot. This is the fleecy fabric that will be soaking up the resin in a moment.

14 You can see that the crossovers have been taped. The capacitor has also been cling-filmed and is getting an application of masking tape. A couple of wooden battens have been glued on to the amp rack at the top and bottom edges to give somewhere for the stretchers to be screwed to.

15 Now that the material has been stretched down over the rack, small strips of wood are screwed into place. This pulls the material under tension and brings out the shape of the equipment underneath.

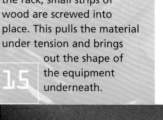

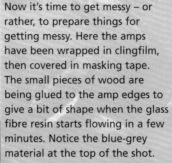

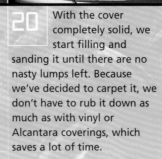

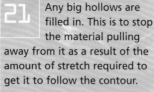

19 More resin is applied to the back and front of the panel until it's thickly coated. Once this has gone completely solid, we can get on with filling the surface to make it smooth enough to cover.

20 With the cover completely solid, we start filling and sanding it until there are no nasty lumps left. Because we've decided to carpet it, we don't have to rub it down as much as with vinyl or Alcantara coverings, which saves a lot of time.

21 Any big hollows are filled in. This is to stop the material pulling away from it as a result of the amount of stretch required to get it to follow the contour.

22 Glass fibre dust can be an irritating menace – literally. Sealing an overall sleeve to a glove with masking tape looks weird but it's effective at keeping the stuff out.

For this final little bit of rubbing down, the glove has gone. Notice that a couple of windows have appeared in the cover to let the Directed badges show through.

23

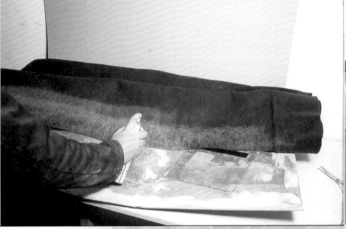

24 Covering a piece this big isn't too bad, so long as you work steadily. Gluing a manageable piece at a time seems to be the best way to go. Then you can flatten out any ripples before you glue some more and work that smooth, too.

25 The last job on the cover is to cut the hole for the boot light. Its wiring is lengthened to allow it to be clipped into the cover.

This is the final effect. Plenty of room for goodies in the boot and an interesting, curvy rack cover.

28

26 This reminds you what we're covering up, and shows the rack finished and painted. Note how short the power lead is from the capacitor to the 600d bass amp. This is always preferable to having a cap fitted miles from the amp it's wired on to.

27 The cover is such a good fit it needs only one screw to hold it tight.

Under-floor equipment racks

To show how to fit a subterranean rack, we thought we'd have a go at some unobtrusive boot builds in a Nissan 200SX. This car is driven daily and used as a camera car, so any audio installation has to take into account the fact the boot is frequently filled to the gills with stepladders, three camera bags, two tripods… You get the idea.

This gives us an immediate problem – how to fit an amp into the section alongside the spare wheel without compromising the amp cooling or subjecting it to the potential of heavy weights being dropped on it. We also wanted to find room for an equaliser. And there's another little problem. We didn't want to drill any holes in the boot floor and so allow rust to get a foothold in the steelwork. We did want them both remain in place should we have an accident, though. So we started scratching our heads and came up with this idea.

01 To get around the tinny sounds coming from the boot, the floor gets a good going over with Dynamat sound deadening. The spare wheel is refitted to give us an idea of just how much room we've got to play with once we start installing with the gear. The left-hand side looks favourite for the amp, while the right-hand side looks just big enough to take the equaliser.

02 You don't need to see another pair of card templates, do you? Good. The floors are cut from 9 mm MDF sheet, while the support rails are chopped from 18 mm MDF. The awkward bit is cutting the profile of the support rail where it fits against the floor of the car. Once this is done, though, the board and rail are glued and nailed together before painting.

To keep it looking tidy, the mounts are sprayed with satin black paint. Once they've dried off, the MDF panels are attached to the car using a construction adhesive called No More Nails. This gives a very strong bond, even between wood and Dynamat, so it's ideal.

03

After pumping a few good blobs on to the underside of the board, it's dropped into place. Then we move it around a little to check the glue is sticking to the floor in enough places to hold the rack solidly. Once the panel is lifted up, the splodges of glue show it has taken hold everywhere we applied it, so we drop the panel back down to get a strong bond. We then do the same thing with the equaliser board.

04

You've seen plenty of wiring by now, so here's the Phoenix Gold XS4600 amp in place and ready to go. It looks big for a 4x25 watt amp, doesn't it? Maybe that's because it can produce a load more than that when there's higher voltage and the impedance has dropped a bit. We must do something about the cooling, though.

05

10

These two arrows show the direction of rotation and the direction of airflow. That's to make sure you get it the right way round when you fit it to your rack.

11

This is where the pipe connects to. It receives air blown into the rack from the fan at the other end of that support bar.

12

And this is where the pipe exits. Behind this trim is the stale air vent. We direct the pipe out through the vent, and the gentle suction of driving the car along draws the warmed air out of the rack. Cool. Literally.

13

Here's the support bar showing both fan and pipe. The wheel well isn't airtight, but as air is pumped into the rack, it gets drawn out through the pipe rather than sitting in the well.

On the other side of the boot, the equaliser goes in easily enough, just needing a few wires to get it going. The four-cable loom you can see sticking from the power plug contains a 12-volt feed and ground, a remote turn-on input, and a delayed remote output. This controls the rest of the components in the system to eliminate turn on-off noise. It works, too.

06

This is the neat sort of effect you should aim for in all your wiring. The grey cable is the LPL-44 connection that gives bass level control from the driver's seat.

07

The signal cables laid out on their way to the amp. They are neat and easy to follow, rather than just wrapped around the spare wheel because no one will see them.

08

A cooling fan and some flexible pipe. Can you guess where they're going?

09

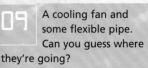

14 The final dressing of the boot floor. And proof that you can get a decent system into a car without taking up masses of room.

15 First the amp cover goes on.

16 The spare wheel cover, complete with support pieces for the equaliser cover.

17 And finally the equaliser disappears from view. Now there's great tunes and still plenty of room for gear.

14 Charge account

If you're adding a fair amount of stereo kit to your car, the charging system will probably struggle to keep up with the extra demands. Unless you look after it, you could find yourself stranded when it lets you down. Which is always late at night, in foul weather, where you have no mobile phone signal.

So let's have a closer look at the vehicle's charging system and see how to upgrade it. But first, there are quite a few things you can do to help its performance, and by doing that, the performance of the stereo, too.

Electrical flow around a circuit has often been likened to water flowing around a plumbing system. Without a pipe to return the flow, a circuit can't be completed so the water doesn't move. And if the pipe is too small, the flow rate will suffer.

In electrical terms, that basically means that if a circuit isn't completed, the item wired in won't work. And if the wire is too small for the current being passed, the item won't perform to its best abilities. This applies to *all* the cabling in the circuit. It's no use running great lumps of 2-gauge cable to power all your amps, but leaving the weedy factory earth cables joining the engine block to the body and to the battery.

While almost everyone can see the need for big, chunky positive cables, the earth cables often get missed out, particularly if they appear to be a decent gauge already. If they are a good size, then there is a lot of current flowing through the vehicle's own system and the manufacturer deemed it necessary to fit the good stuff. But since you are adding a load more current-shifting capability, you should upgrade that cable so all that extra current can get through.

The reason for upgrading the cable is internal resistance. Just as pressure builds up when lots of water goes down a thin pipe, so resistance builds up when lots of current goes down a thin cable. This results in the voltage dropping off before it reaches the equipment, and can have dire results for the stereo and the car.

This increased resistance shows itself as heat and a puny cable

Go to town on your battery and wiring, and you might as well display it like this.

trying to pass large amounts of current will get warm. If the problem isn't attended to, there's every chance that the wire will melt its insulation and short out – or in very serious cases it could set the insulation on fire.

To decide which gauge of cable is needed, see Table 1. This shows the gauge required to flow various amounts of current over several distances. Once you've found out how far you want to run the power lead, you need to know what the current draw of your system is, and then cross-refer that to see which size of cable is required.

So how do you figure out your system's current consumption? Let's say our hypothetical system runs three amps, which have a total power output of 600 watts. That's based on the continous ratings, not the peaks, and it takes into account the loading of the speaker system, too.

Then we have to account for the amplifiers' efficiency, which is generally accepted as 50 per cent. So to produce 600 watts, the

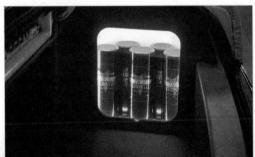

A bank of stiffening capacitors can help to keep the juice flowing to your amplifiers when the bass really starts pounding.

Table 1

Power Cable Calculator
Length in feet for 0.5-volt loss

Amperes Gauge	20	30	40	50	60	75	100	150	200	500	750
00							57	38	29	11	08
0						61	45	30	23	09	06
1					60	48	36	24	18	07	X
2				57	48	38	29	19	14	X	X
3			57	45	38	30	23	15	11	X	X
4		60	45	36	30	24	18	12	09	X	X
5	71	48	36	29	24	19	14	10	07	X	X
6	57	38	28	23	19	15	11	08	X	X	X
7	45	30	22	18	15	12	09	X	X	X	X
8	36	24	18	14	12	09	X	X	X	X	X
9	28	19	14	11	09	X	X	X	X	X	X
10	22	15	11	09	X	X	X	X	X	X	X
12	14	09	07	X	X	X	X	X	X	X	X

The wire must not fall on the X part of the chart, indicating that the current exceeds the capacity of the wire, no matter how short the wire. The wire must not be any longer than shown on the rest of the chart.

amps will also waste 600 watts, so we have to calculate the current consumption on the 1200 watt total figure.

To err on the safe side, let's say that the vehicle system runs on 12.6 volts, which is a fully charged battery's nominal reading. We divide 1200 by 12.6 and come up with a current consumption figure of 95.24 amperes. By looking at the chart and finding 100 amps on the top line, we can follow that column down until we get to the right cable length.

If our hypothetical car needs a 15 ft run of cable, we can see that we require a longer run than is acceptable in 5-gauge, but we're far enough inside the maximum length of 4-gauge to use that. So, armed with that knowledge, we should be able to install the correct cable to allow the stereo to work to its maximum. Just don't forget to upgrade the earth cable between the battery, car body and engine block, and you'll be fine.

But what if you've uprated your supply and ground cables, and you're still flattening batteries and slowing down your wipers when the bass cuts in? Let's have a quick look at the components

of the vehicle's charging system to see what they do and how they do it.

The charging system basically consists of the current-producing device and the storage medium – or alternator and battery. Dead easy. Some classic vehicles may still have dynamos, but for our purposes we'll just be dealing with alternators.

The alternator is driven by a belt, which is wrapped around a pulley on the engine's crankshaft, and produces current. Higher engine speeds result in higher outputs, but alternators are pretty efficient at lower revs – hence their suitability for modern road conditions, where cars spend ages stuck in traffic jams with their lights, heated rear windows and other current-draining accessories switched on.

The alternator, as its name suggests, produces alternating current – AC – rather than the direct current that the vehicle's systems can deal with. So the alternator has a built-in rectifier that produces DC from the AC. This process leaves a very small AC component within the DC flow, known as AC ripple. This isn't damaging to any of the car's systems, but it can sometimes be heard as noise. Thankfully, the battery is a good ripple filter, so generally this noise shouldn't get through.

The voltage regulator defines the amount of current actually produced, and this checks the charge level of the battery and adjusts the output accordingly. Most alternators have this regulator built in, and it's non-adjustable.

Bigger, aftermarket alternators are normally supplied with an outboard regulator that is adjustable, which allows the charge rate to be altered according to the needs of the car. Mounting the regulator outside the alternator also has the benefit of keeping it cool, which is always a good idea when dealing with electrical devices.

The charge rate metered by the regulator is important because batteries can be damaged by being over-charged. Much more than 15 volts for any length of time can boil off the electrolyte in the individual cells, causing early failure of the battery, which won't hold a charge.

Modern batteries used for vehicle systems are almost exclusively lead-acid types, either open-celled or closed-cell. Closed-cell batteries are often known as maintenance-free because the cells can't be topped up with distilled water. But they can still be overcharged and boil dry just like the open-cell variety, so don't think that they are sealed up tight and safe to use rolling around the interior of the car.

The car's battery has a couple of tasks to perform. The main one is to hold the power necessary to start the engine. It isn't really there to power the car's electrical systems at all, apart from when the engine is switched off. That's the job of the alternator, which operates at a slightly higher voltage level than the battery.

To be charged successfully, a battery needs to receive at least 1.2 volts more than its normal output voltage, and in a regular lead-acid car battery this figure is around 12.6 volts. So the alternator needs to kick out something over 13.8 volts to keep the car's system happy and the battery topped off.

How does this affect the average car audio fan, and their car and system? Does it matter if the car still starts and seems to run fine, even with the stereo pumping all the time? Well, yes, it does matter, and here's why.

When the vehicle manufacturer designs a charging system for a car, it leaves only a limited amount of spare capacity after all the possible electrical drains have been calculated. You're probably

If you can squeeze an extra battery under the bonnet, why not make a feature of it?

Not only is this battery and capacitor display fantastic to look at, those solid blocks of machined perspex make it ultra safe.

aware that some more highly specified models have a bigger alternator and battery than their mundane cousins, and this is why. More electrical toys need more juice.

So when you add a decent car stereo with a couple of amps eating large and continuous amounts of current, there's often a shortfall in the charging system's ability to supply the new equipment and still keep the battery sufficiently topped up. Have you ever have driven at night with the headlights and stereo on, watching the dash lights flickering a bit in time with the bass notes? That's why.

To find out what kind of extra weight you're putting on to the electrical system of a vehicle, just do the same sum as for checking cable gauges. This simple arithmetic should make it clear that if a car has a reasonably powerful system, the alternator and battery are hanging by a thread.

It's a good idea to fit an uprated alternator and an extra battery

If you want to keep things looking really factory under your bonnet, you could hide your fuseholder in something like this relay box on a Vauxhall Vectra.

to keep the stereo going. To get the best performance from the additional battery, it needs to be as close as possible in capacity and condition to the vehicle's original item. For most cars, this means getting a pair of identical batteries so that they are both in peak condition and offer a similar load for the alternator. Imagine what would happen if you had a tiny car battery and a fork-lift truck battery in the spare wheel well to run the stereo. The alternator regulator wouldn't know what to do.

Having decided to double up on the battery capacity with a pair of well-matched lead-acid cells, how do they get joined together? There are a couple of options, but only one really makes sense.

The simplest way to join the cells is to run a piece of wire from the front battery positive to the rear battery positive, and

complete the circuit by earthing the new one to the body. Job done. The main problem with this is that there's no way to isolate the two batteries and prevent the stereo from draining the car's cell when the engine isn't running but the system is being cranked. How daft would you feel needing a jump start having spent an hour impressing all your mates down at the Drive-Thru?

This need to break the connection between the two cells is catered for by a couple of products that have been available for years. Looking at the problem closely, though, one is definitely more suitable than the other.

One of the most widely used items is a Multiple Battery Isolator, and you've probably seen cars fitted with them. Many are based around a big piece of heatsink with three terminals on the top for the alternator input and the two isolated outputs for the car and stereo batteries. They contain heavy-duty diodes that pass current in one direction only, so breaking the connection between the two batteries.

The main flaw with these is the diodes themselves. These are like electrical one-way valves, but they also take a little voltage from the flow going through them. To make matters worse, as they heat up, this voltage penalty increases. The minimum price to pay is 0.7 volts – it's just one of those physics things – and it's possible for that figure to rise to more than 1.5 volts as the diodes continue to heat up.

While you're thinking about that, remember that the alternator had to produce a 1.2 volt minimum to charge the battery in the first place, and you can see that the multi-isolator can be a bit of a nightmare in a bigger system. So what's the alternative?

Basically it's a relay – bigger and more robust than the little ones you use to switch spotlights and trigger stereo components, but exactly the same in principle. (Chapter Eight explains relays in greater depth.) A Multiple Battery Contacter (MBC), as it's known, is a very heavily rated relay that will join two or more batteries together without suffering any voltage loss. And it will break that connection quickly and easily with the minimum of extra wiring.

But before you rush out to your local motorist discount store to get a car starter solenoid instead, be warned. An MBC is designed to take large amounts of current passing through it for hours on end, and the energiser coil doesn't melt when it's powered up for long periods.

A starter solenoid is designed to pass a huge current for a short burst, but it will give up the ghost if connected for any length of time. And don't go looking at the current rating and think that it will be okay for your system. The rating is based on what the unit can pass for that very short period, not continuously. Because you are dealing with something that can affect your safety as well as the stereo, use the proper thing.

To maximise the performance of your new alternator/extra battery combo, and to keep it safe, where should the new battery go? Well, common sense says that fitting it near to the amplifiers cuts down on wire runs, so normally the boot is favourite. This is a good place to fit it, but there are a couple of safety implications.

The main one is sealing the battery from the airspace inside the car. If the regulator fails and the battery is over-charged, the vented electrolyte gas will need to go somewhere – and into the passenger compartment isn't the best place at all. Even having it going into the boot is a bad plan, because the gas is both corrosive *and* explosive.

It's much better to mount the battery in a sealed box with a vent pipe running outside the car. Because the battery is such a heavy piece of kit, make sure the box is fitted securely, otherwise some enthusiastic cornering could end up with the battery on its side and acid sloshing about on the boot floor.

The final point to think about is fusing. The cable that runs the length of the car from battery to battery should be fused at both ends. There's at least one metal bulkhead and numerous edges for that cable to pass over, so the dual fuses are a must.

That way, if there's a short anywhere on the line, both fuses will blow and leave the cable safe. Fuse only one end and the other battery will dump all its current into the short circuit. That will result in some expensive damage as the cable becomes white hot and tries to burn through everything it touches. Then you'll be checking out the 'fire' section of your insurance policy…

Finally, don't think that because one extra battery is a good idea, ten must be brilliant. You can add too many batteries to the point where the alternator can't keep them charged up even before you've turned on the stereo. If you want to fill a van full of batteries, you'd better fill the engine bay with alternators, too.

Watts next?

Let's have a go at a charging system upgrade and an auxiliary battery install. We're putting the new gear on to a MkII VW Golf GTI that's been treated to a few other stereo bits, so the car does need the surgery. And because it has done a few miles and the alternator is the original one from new, it's time this was swapped anyway.

The 55 amp unit is making way for a 95 amp Audi alternator, so there'll be plenty of reserve current to keep the batteries and everything else in the best of health. While we're under the bonnet, the build that will hold the battery contacter and the first system supply fuse will be made, and all the cabling associated with the charging and starting circuit will be uprated, too.

Protecting cable when it goes through any steelwork areas of your car is absolutely vital, using something like this hard plastic split loom tube. And don't forget the gaffa tape to stop your wiring going walkabout.

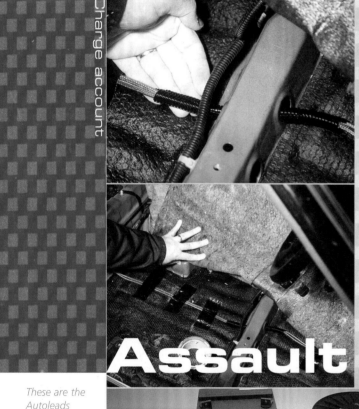

Assault and battery

These are the Autoleads goodies we're going to use to fit our secondary battery system.

01 The first job is to disconnect the battery. It sounds obvious, but if you started playing around with the alternator before disconnecting the other end of the main feed cable, the results could be shocking. And costly. So with the battery lead removed, the job starts properly.

If your vehicle is newer than this one, check if anything else has to be done when disconnecting the battery. A lot of modern cars don't like the battery being flattened or undone because it can freak out something in its brain and cause hiccups when you reconnect things later. Check your handbook, Haynes manual or dealer to save yourself any problems.

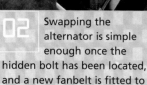

02 Swapping the alternator is simple enough once the hidden bolt has been located, and a new fanbelt is fitted to be on the safe side. The belt tension is adjusted correctly to give the best charging output, and then we can start on the rest of the job.

The output stud on the back of the Golf's new alternator is big enough to accept an 8.3 mm ring terminal attached to the new main power cable that we're going to make up. This cable links together the alternator output stud and the starter motor terminal, and another joins this to the battery clamp. In a similar way, the earth circuit is linked from battery to bodywork, and then from there to the gearbox/engine assembly. The old wiring looks awfully thin, so the new four-gauge stuff will be a big improvement. The new cables are being made from Autoleads 4-gauge cable.

03 The length of the new cables is checked against their proposed route, and then cut with the heavy-duty cutting section of some large terminal crimping pliers.

Once the length is copied from the original piece, the new ring terminals are crimped on with the same pair of pliers, which are designed to cope with this size of connector.

04

05 Here's the neatly crimped result.

For added security and current capability, we very carefully solder the terminal as well, using a blowtorch with a fine flame...

06

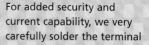

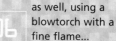

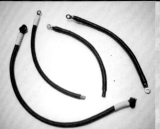

09 The main lead from alternator to starter also has a couple of stud boots fitted to cover up the live terminals once the lead is in place. These are pretty fiddly to get on, being a very tight fit, and also quite inflexible. By warming them up with a heat gun, they become flexible enough to slide over the cable, helped by a little silicon spray.

For added protection, we cover the cables in convoluted tubing. On the main positive cable, the boots are slid over the ring terminals so that the tubing goes right up to the terminal joint, and more heatshrink makes the whole thing weatherproof. More gentle heat will be applied to the boots when the cable is refitted so that the nuts can be accessed and tightened easily.

07 ...and plenty of solder. A blowtorch is the only thing hot enough to heat this amount of wire, but you must be careful not to melt the insulation, or your fingers. You must make sure that this joint is well made or there might be starting and charging problems.

08 Next we colour-code the finished cables with heatshrink. In this case we're using yellow for positive and black for negative, to match the cosmetics of the car.

14 The hole for the battery contacter is the next thing to cut out.

15 Now the contacter relay can be attached from underneath so that just the bolt heads remain visible.

16 The new power cable that leads from the battery to the starter motor can be fitted.

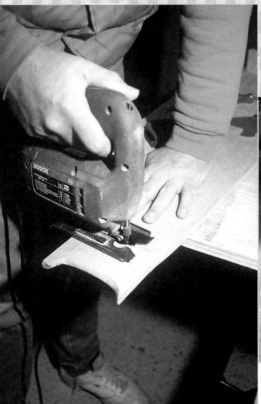

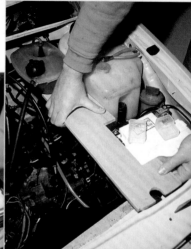

11 This lets you attach all the vehicle cables to the block as well, making good connections to all the vehicle systems. Just one word of caution, though. The terminals can be tightened up very tightly, so make sure you brace the terminal post before leaning too hard on the spanner. It's surprisingly easy to crack the complete lead terminal off the battery body if you aren't careful.

12 Fitting the battery contacter and main fuseholder is the next job. An MDF mounting is made to fit between the slam panel and the expansion tank using a contour gauge to get the right shape.

13 The panel is checked for fit, and it will be bolted in place at both ends.

10 Battery terminations are looked after by the large Autoleads Mega terminal blocks, which take cables directly into their body rather than relying on ring terminals being held under bolts.

You can see the terminal boot covering the solenoid stud for added protection.

17

The alternator output stud, covered by the other protective boot.

18

The battery terminals are equally well protected by these rubber covers once the cables are fitted.

19

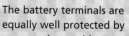

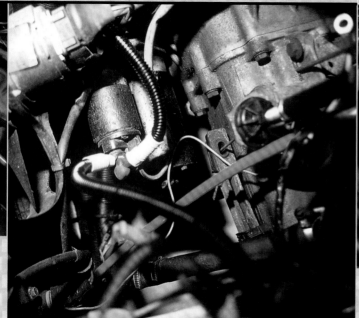

20 Behind the battery is the ground point where the new earth cables are fitted, with a new bolt.

21 The main power cable can be pulled up through the MDF panel on its way to the fuseholder.

22 The fuseholder and battery contacter are connected with a short length of 4-gauge cable.

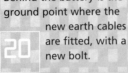
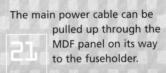
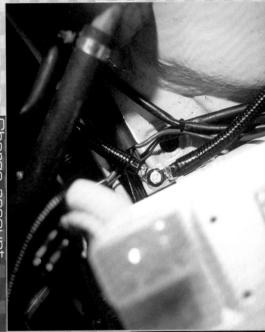

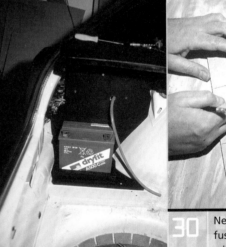

27 To blend into the cosmetic theme, the battery tray is painted black before fitting it into the car.

28 The support fits into the back of the Golf with a couple of screws, which go into an internal panel rather than through to the outside of the car. This stops any rust getting hold of the holes.

29 The second battery fits easily into the tray. Now it needs to be secured so that it can't jump out under any circumstances.

30 Next, make the fuseholder panel that will keep the battery in place. It's cut from 9 mm MDF, and here are the main fuse and equipment fuses and earth block being laid out.

The main cable from the contacter to the rear battery runs through a waterproof body gland in the bulkhead, and it's protected by more split loom tube on its journey through the car. Cable ties are used to hold it in place in the engine bay, stopping it getting caught up in anything that moves.

23

The main power cable comes out behind the area where the second battery is going to go.

24

The second battery support is made from MDF and wood battens...

25

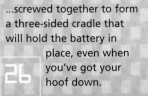

...screwed together to form a three-sided cradle that will hold the battery in place, even when you've got your hoof down.

26

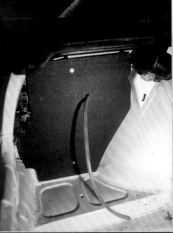

The holes for the wires are drilled before the panel is painted black and fitted to the car.

31

With the panel in place, the wiring can be terminated to go on to the new battery. Notice that the fuse panel has locked the battery down into the tray. The only way to take the battery out will be to undo the wiring and then remove the fuse panel before lifting the battery out of the tray.

32

Once the battery is connected, the contacter needs a couple of additional wires to control when it comes in. On the Golf, this means finding an ignition feed that cuts in only when the engine runs, so that the batteries are disconnected from each other when the engine is switched off.

The additional cell we're using is a Sonnenschein Dry Fit battery designed for golf cart use. We went for one of these mainly because it's a recombinant gas battery that is sealed and shouldn't leak any fumes or electrolyte into the interior of the boot. The battery compartment will have a vent pipe fitted, just in case, but there shouldn't be any problems unless the charging system has a fit and decides to throw out more than 16.5 volts, which is very unlikely.

The earth termination is taken up behind the rear side panel, where there is a good chance of getting a solid ground connection without inducing any rust formation by drilling through to the outside of the car. An Autoleads ground terminal is bolted to the steel panel and the 4-gauge earth cable held under the Allen bolt. After the bolts are tightened, the surrounding area is treated with anti-rust compound to stop any possible oxidisation of the metalwork. And that's it.

Even the simplest head unit, amp and speaker combo needs to be tweaked correctly to get the best from it. If you don't bother, you'll be wasting the money you've spent on your new gear, and you'll be wasting the gear itself. So it's vital to get the kit set up properly, but where do you start?

15 Sound check

"I'll have a choc-ice and a 99 please - oh, and one of those Calippos..."

This testing should be done with the engine switched off, so make sure your battery is well charged. And don't expect to be able to sit in your car for hours. When you start listening critically, you need to do short stints so that you can tell when something has changed – for better or worse – rather than sitting there until you don't know what's going on.

On a simple system with minimal tweakable controls, all you can do is ensure the amplifier gain is set properly for the head unit, and then possibly play around with the wiring of the front speakers to see if any improvements can be made by altering their polarity.

Sound Offs are a sort of motorsport. Motorsport is dangerous. Here's a van eating some men. (Actually, they're looking at digital displays which are difficult to read in sunlight.)

Simple settings

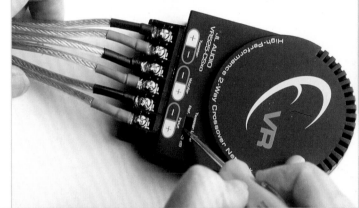

To set up an amp, first make sure the gain control is turned all the way down. Then all you have to do is stick a pretty dynamic recording into your head unit and turn the volume up to about the three-quarter mark. If you want more noise, just turn up the gain on the amp until you get the beginnings of distortion coming through the speakers, then turn it down a tad from there. If any hiss has started to come through, back the amp off a bit more until it disappears, and you're done.

01 To improve the sound quality and possibly the staging of the system – assuming you're running the basic amp, fronts, and subs system – about all you've got to play with is the polarity of the front speakers and, if your passive crossovers have one, the tweeter level control.

Before you go messing with them, play some music, sit back, close your eyes and listen to where the sound's coming from. If it's more or less in the centre of the car, leave things alone because that's what we want.

If the music appears to come from your side of the car, with a little bit happening on the far side, you'll probably get an improvement by flipping the polarity of the far-side speakers. You have the choice of swapping just the mid, just the tweeter, or both drivers together. If you have a passive crossover with screw terminals, it's easier if you swap things over there, rather than having to do it at the speaker.

02 Change the positive and negative wires from one speaker at a time – that is, put the negative on the positive terminal and the positive on the negative terminal. Then listen to detect if there's an improvement, and that the sound is coming from across the front of the car. You can try all three different swaps to see which improves things the most because you won't damage anything by doing it. Just be careful not to accidentally short out any feed wires or you could do something a nasty.

By reversing the polarity of one or both of the speakers on one side of the car, you bring their output back into phase at your listening position. If the sounds are in phase, you should get a realistic representation of what was recorded on to your CD in the studio. If they'e out of phase, they can sound unfocussed and thinned out.

03 The tweeter level control allows you to turn the tweeters down in relation to the mid range drivers on a permanent basis, rather than just knocking the treble down on the head unit. If the tweeters point directly at you or are much nearer than the mids, this may be beneficial. You can also try altering the tweeter mounting angle to see if that improves the way the music is reproduced. So have an experiment and learn what each alteration does to the sound, and whether it's better or not.

If you have a more complicated install, you'll find there's a lot more to setting the levels than just winding the gain up until something starts crackling. You really need to get hold of an oscilloscope and someone who knows how to use it to set the system up properly. This assumes that the dealer you bought the kit from has these amenities to hand.

If you have to do this on your own, follow the instructions on each piece of kit to the letter and you should be okay. Most manufacturers of serious equipment provide good manuals that go through set-up in logical stages, so you shouldn't have too many problems.

04 If you go back to the dealer, he or she will probably wheel out a Real Time Analyser (RTA), which can be extremely useful for pinpointing problems in your system's frequency response. It will show you what your system is doing as a line of dots or columns – depending on make of RTA – and this makes the position of the peaks and troughs obvious.

05 The RTA uses a microphone that is placed at about head height, so it picks up the sound the same way as you hear it. Pink noise is played through the system, which means that every frequency from 20Hz to 20kHz should be there in equal amounts. The display on the screen shows what's missing or what's too dominant.

If you have an equaliser, you can attack the high and low points to smooth things out, but there are a few things to be aware of. Firstly, your brain will notice peaks a lot more than troughs, so boosting a low point to try to get it to rise into line might not be as necessary as you'd think. Try dropping the high points first to see if things look – and sound – smoother.

Secondly, boosting a low point with an equaliser means you are introducing gain into a particular frequency band. That might overload a component that's downstream of the equaliser and bring in audible distortion. Since you equalise a system after you've set up the gains, boosting anything too much can have nasty effects on what you hear.

06 Finally, there is no such thing as an ideal curve. You might prefer your music played in a different way to the person who's trying to set it up, so make sure you listen as you tweak.

It's a good idea to get the equaliser on your lap during set-up sessions. This often isn't easy because the unit will be built into somewhere that's inaccessible from the driver's seat, but you can get round this.

How **loud** is it, mister?

An RTA can tell you how loud your system is. It's all very well to be able to turn it up and wobble your mirror, but when someone asks you the question, you need to know.

If you've put the system together to go as loud as possible, you should test it on a meter with a microphone that can accept high pressure inputs so you don't do it any damage. Special high-volume meters can take more than 170 dB inputs, so you shouldn't damage them unless you've got a competition-only monster – complete with bullet-proof glass, concrete-filled floors and enough power to support the National Grid.

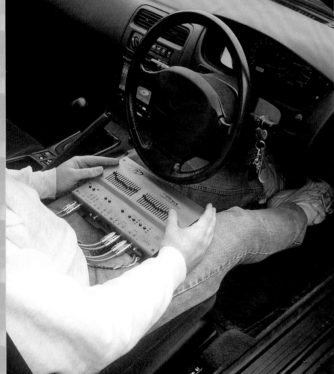

07 Make up a set of leads that allow you to remove the equaliser from its usual home, and feed them through to where you're sitting. If two RCA leads go to the EQ, you need two long signal leads – with sockets at one end and plugs at the other – and a power/earth/remote lead to extend the 12-volt feeds. Then you – or the shop's tweaker – can sit and alter settings to your heart's content. Just do it in short bursts of about 20 minutes so you can detect the changes properly.

If you want to get really into tweaking, buy some audiophile test discs as well as some good recordings of music. Also, go to hear some live music so you know what you're trying to recreate. It'll make it easier if you do.

What's that **noise?**

Then there's interference, but if you follow the basic rules of fitting and cable running, you should have a noise-free system.

The main things are to keep cable runs far enough away from vehicle looms not to pick up anything from them; get a really good system earth point; and have a battery that's in good condition. If you have all these points covered, you should be laughing.

If you do have noise, there are a few things that will help eliminate it before you trek back to the dealer and ask for help. First you need to know what sort of noise it is.

If it's a low crackling that speeds up when you rev the engine, it's probably coming from the ignition circuit. If it's a high-pitched whine that also goes up and down according to revs, it's most likely to be from the alternator. A high-pitched whine that stays constant regardless of revs is probably the fuel pump.

If you're absolutely sure you aren't running a cable close enough to anything to pick up noise – and you've tried moving cables closer to and further from other looms on the vehicle's floor to check the effect – any one of these noises can be caused by a bad earth on some part of your installation. If you've hooked up to the factory head unit wiring, it could be the earth point that's been used under the dash for that, or maybe the power feed is running close to something else in the dash.

In that case, you should try loosely wiring the head unit up to the same feed and earth points used for the rest of the system. If the noise goes, make a neat job of running the necessary cables out of sight and reassemble the car. If that doesn't cure it, start isolating components until you find the one where the noise is coming into the signal chain, and try rewiring that.

After you've gone through re-earthing and feeding each individual component, you might have to attack the offending item on the car. There's always the possibility that something has broken down and needs replacing to cure the problem. If so, you should contact your audio supplier or main dealer.

Almost regardless of the kind of car audio system you install, you should make sure you add some form of protection to the vehicle. Just like stereo gear, there are a whole host of security products out there. To help you decide what you need, this what they do.

To get theft cover from your insurance company, the chances are that your car will need to have some form of immobiliser – and most likely it will have to be up to Thatcham specifications.

That's alarming

The best deterrent against little toe-rags breaking into your car is a dog that would rip their arms off. Or, in the case of Lily here, one that would lick them to death.

'Thatcham-approved' means the alarm or immobiliser has been scrutinised by the insurance industry's testing engineers and meets the strict guidelines they've laid down. They've set standards for alarms, immobilisers and mechanical locking devices.

Mechanical devices range from things you carry around in the car and then slip over the gearlever, steering wheel or pedals, right up to movable posts that stop your car from being moved off your property in the first place. Obviously, these posts aren't any use when you've driven into town to go clubbing, but they are very effective when you're at home. And a good steering-wheel cover or gearlever lock can be a very effective deterrent against someone who wants a lift home without asking you.

An immobiliser does exactly what it says on the box. It stops the vehicle from being started by cutting two or three vital circuits, such as ignition, fuel pump and starter. These can only be reconnected when the appropriate key or code is inserted, waved near or tapped in to the receiver; then the ignition key will start the car as usual. Most of these devices carry no siren facility, so if someone breaks in and has a go at nicking your music, no one is usually the wiser. Which is great if anyone takes any notice.

Alarm systems are the next level up from immobilisers, and their mission is to stop someone entering your car in the first place. If someone tries, the alarm will flash the car's lights and make a shed-load of noise. The only problem is that most car alarms are ignored because so many false-alarm so much of the time.

The best you can hope for is to be close enough to hear it scream so that you can go and see what's happening. What you do then is another thing entirely, and several people have been injured or killed trying to stop car thieves from nicking their motors, so act cautiously if you do decide to go back to your car when you hear it wailing. At least thieves don't like the noise of a siren and are likely to leg it should the alarm go off, so alarms are well worth having.

Even if you have an approved device already fitted to your motor, there are still things you can do to prevent your car being considered as a target for thieves. When you have to leave your car at night, make sure you park it near a street lamp. Thieves like darkness, so make sure your motor's well lit. Park with other vehicles so that there is plenty of pedestrian movement, because crooks prefer peace and quiet.

Make sure you remove anything that looks nickable from the car's cabin and leave it in the boot. It's common sense, but you still see people leaving CDs, expensive jackets and bags in full view.

If you're going to shift stuff out of sight, try to do it before you park up, or at least don't get out of the car with all your goodies and then stash them in the boot under the watchful gaze of the local villlains. They'll be into your boot before you're 500 metres away and, even if you've got an alarm, they'll be on their way with something before you can leg it back.

Since aftermarket alarms have popularised convenience features such as central door locking, some people think that the remote central locking system on their car must be attached to some form

of security. Not always. And while they may be oblivious to the fact that there isn't an alarm tucked away in their pride and joy, most car thieves know exactly what the score is.

This situation has brought about an increase in add-on alarm modules that interface with the original locking system. When the remote control triggers the door locks, the alarm is automatically set; when the doors are unlocked, the alarm is disabled. These tend to be fairly inexpensive units that give basic security cover, but it's better than nothing. If you do have a factory-fitted remote door-lock system, it's worth checking to see if there *really* is an alarm hooked up to it.

Most people ignore an alarm siren because there are so many false alarms. And most false triggers come from the unit being badly fitted or incorrectly set up. In this respect, alarm systems are very different from audio systems, so we don't recommend that you buy your own and have a go at installing it if you've never done anything like it before.

The main reason for this is one of the biggest differences between stereos and security products – namely, the alarm has to be accurately wired into several vehicle circuits to ensure that it gets the correct information about the status of the car. A stereo, on the other hand, requires only its main power feed and a switched feed to operate when the ignition is turned on. Apart from that, and the occasional illumination supply, the stereo is pretty much self-contained.

A good alarm fitter will be well used to setting security systems to be as reliable as possible. If you're doing it only once every couple of years when you change your car, you'll never get familiar enough with the system and all its little foibles.

Even though we don't recommend that the inexperienced should fit an alarm, it's still important to know what's available, how it works and what to look for when shopping round to get your security gear fitted.

If your insurance company tells you to get a Thatcham-approved product, a lot of the units will be off-limits. You can still have a

choice over what extras you get, but underneath it all will be an approved kit.

If you don't have to toe the line, you can choose from a wider range of products, and they can have features that Thatcham won't allow. A valet option allows you to park your car without the alarm being set, which can be useful when you are working on the car, or just washing and cleaning it out. A Thatcham unit can only be set into valet for one cycle of key-on-key-off so if you start the engine and then stop it again, you'll have to reset it into valet. It isn't as convenient, but means you don't forget to set the alarm.

Apart from choosing the main brain and picking which functions you require, you can also add on sensors and modules to give control over other vehicle systems. Alarms now wind up electric windows, move electric seats and mirrors, and can even open boots and bonnets, all from a press of a button. This looks particularly good when you park up somewhere, jump out of the car and then it closes the windows and sunroof, and locks the door as you walk away.

A remote starter facility is even more cool. This means you can fire up the engine as you walk up to the car for maximum posing. Or you can start the motor on a cold day and have it defrosting itself before you've finished your breakfast, without leaving the house. And if anyone tries to steal it, the engine will cut out and the alarm will sound. How swish is that?

Additional sensors can also cover other forms of vehicle intrusion or attack, and you can even protect soft-top cars which are parked with their roof down. For instance, a microwave sensor can pick up a disturbance in the vehicle interior but isn't triggered by the wind.

An anti-hijack feature is comparatively new but it's becoming more popular. It means you can give up the car to anyone who threatens you, but if he or she doesn't punch in the correct code while driving away, the car will glide to a halt once the engine revs drop to a safe level. So they should get far enough away to not come back to beat the code out of you, but they don't get away with the car, either.

You can also buy sensors that detect if your vehicle is being jacked up as someone tries to nick your alloys, but it won't false-alarm if a bus drives by too quickly and rocks the car with the bow wave. Sensors are becoming increasingly sophisticated and can discriminate between actual attacks and possible triggers, but they are only as good as the installation.

We reckon you should leave it to someone who fits them all day long. It also gives you some comeback should you get problems.

Competitive spirit

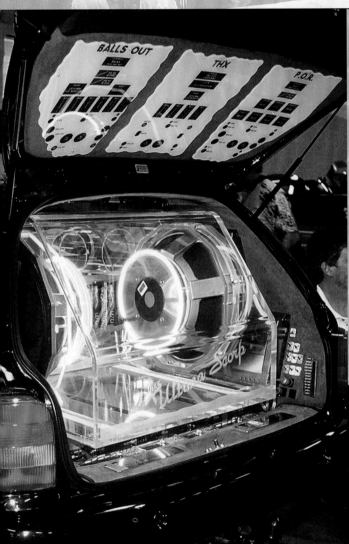

Car stereo equipment and installation techniques have improved dramatically over the past few years. There are so many add-ons available now that you can have the electronic world at your fingertips.

If you really want, you can turn your car into a mobile office, with a computer, e-mail, fax machine and more, all lovingly fitted in leather-covered cabinets that remind you of the office you thought you'd just left. But where's the fun in that? Let's keep work at work, not on the road.

Most people who get into car audio never scale the dizzy heights that can be reached, but there are plenty who go as far as they can to make their car stereo as good, or as loud, or as mental as possible. And if you get any of the car stereo magazines, you're bound to see cars with big installs, lots of custom work and acres of fancy trimming.

So apart from convincing your mates that you're an audio nutter, what can you do with a system that does the business and looks the part? Simple. You can compete against other people who think a lot like you and want to improve their installations through friendly competition.

Every new Sound Off season brings a whole load of new faces in the Novice divisions, eager to show off their cars and the handiwork that's gone into them.

If you're up for it, first choose which competition discipline to enter. The Sound Quality divisions are for those who are constantly trying to perfect the sound of their tunes. Head for SPL if loudness is your thing.

Two organisations currently look after UK competitions and one of them runs both formats. The Sound Challenge Association (SCA) holds competitions at motor-related shows so there's plenty to look around once you've been judged. They are affiliated to the International Auto Sound Challenge Association (IASCA) in the US and use their rules for the Sound Quality (SQ) contests.

If you fancy doing the noisy stuff, SCA runs a head-to-head format called dB Drag Racing. This is the same competition style as the UK dB Drag Racing organisation runs, so you can compete at two lots of shows during the season.

DB Drag Racing contests are run on a simple knockout formula, and all the cars who qualify in a class are brought through in pairs, with the winner from each pairing working their way up to a final.

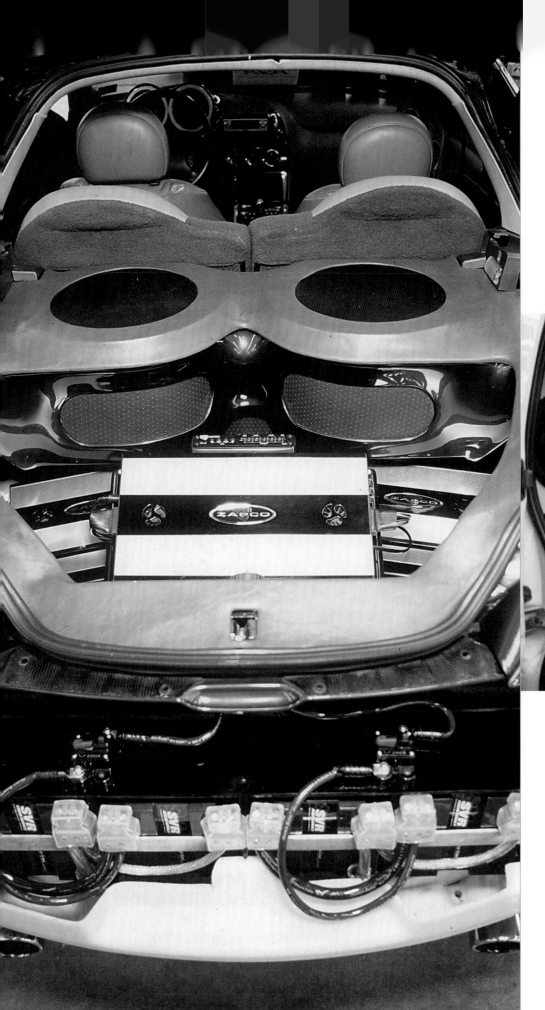

In both organisations' shows, the entrants are split up into different classes based on various criteria. In the SQ contests, there are two distinct levels of competition – Street and Ultimate.

The Street category caters for the first-timer who wants to see how well they get on with a more-simple daily-driver-type system rather than one designed and installed purely for competitive use. Street systems just have to be safe and solidly fitted, and then it's all about how they sound.

The Ultimate division uses a more involved scoresheet, which goes into far more detail about the way the equipment is installed and gives points for creativity, craftsmanship and so on. Both formats are then broken down into classes for Novice, Amateur and Professional, which are further split by amplifier power capability. So there's bound to be a category for you.

The main thing to remember is that, unless you're very well off and can afford a car for competition use only, you'll be using your system much more than the judges. So it makes sense to have something that you enjoy playing and listening to, but that can

also satisfy the judging criteria when it goes into competition. Also, don't think it's just about money. Blank cheque installs are few and far between.

If you're pretty serious about competing in one discipline or the other, you should join the appropriate organisation and get hold of an up-to-date rulebook. Without that, you'll struggle to do what's needed to score well.

If you decide to get a dealer to help you, or to do the installation if you aren't willing or capable to do it yourself, find one with either competition experience or enthusiasm and the interest to read the rulebook with you. It takes time to get the installation right and they'll have to be prepared to put the extra hours in.

When people drop out after a couple of shows, it's often because they've used the wrong dealer. The judges find areas of the sound or installation that could be improved, but the dealer who's taken the money for the initial design and fitting doesn't know what to do to put things right. The competitor is faced with a strip-down and refit – at additional cost – or giving up. It's sad, but it happens every year, so choose your dealer carefully.

Once you get your system finished and down to the show, you'll be expected to present your car in a pristine condition. It might sound strange when the competition is a *Sound* Off, but scores get very close sometimes and occasionally the final decider could be the quality of the presentation.

As a contestant, you're given five minutes to describe your system to the installation judge or judges. Then they'll go through your car thoroughly, checking what's been done against the way it should have been done. Then the sound judges will have a listen to the test disc and mark what they hear appropriately.

After it's been judged and you've got a scoresheet, ask the judges exactly what they meant and why you lost your points. No one else knows what the comments mean apart from the bods who wrote them, and just throwing the judging sheet in the back of the car and heading home won't give you an idea of what's needed to get your system to be the best it can.

Even though it can be a bit stressful getting the car ready and having it judged, Sound Offs are fun events, and meeting lots of like-minded people stops you feeling quite so weird in the real world. Just remember that there's no reason why your car can't do what you want as well as what the judges want, so get out there and enjoy it.

Contact the SCA on 07074 722722 and www.scauk.co.uk, or UK dB Drag Racing on 01923 350928 or through the www.ukdbdrag.com website. They'll give you the full SP on the classes and what competitions are planned.

Glossary

This glossary is aimed at the car audio field, so if a term has been hijacked from another branch of audio or electronics, we've given the car-related meaning. Read on to impress your friends with your new vocabulary and to ensure that no dealer is ever able to baffle you with jargon again.

AC (Alternating Current)
Domestic power supply is alternating current, rather than the DC or direct current your car uses.

Acoustic Short-Circuit
Where a poorly sealed or located loudspeaker or baffle allows front and rear radiated acoustic information to cancel each other.

Acoustic-Suspension Enclosure
A sealed speaker box that uses the air pressure inside the box to augment the speaker's own suspension.

Active Crossover (Active Dividing Network)
An electronic device that divides the audio signal from a source component into different frequency bands, such as sub bass, mid range and treble, *before* they are amplified. They are used in multi-channel systems.

Aftermarket
Generally used to mean non-standard equipment added to a vehicle by someone other than the manufacturer or dealer.

Alternator
The alternator generates the electrical power for the vehicle, keeping the battery topped up and powering all the vehicle's systems. It produces alternating current (AC) which is converted – or rectified – into direct current (DC) by the rectifier.

Alternator Whine
High-frequency interference, produced by the alternator, that is heard over the stereo system. The pitch rises and falls with the engine revs and, depending on severity, it can either be heard between tracks when there's no music present, or it can obliterate the music at any level.

Ambience
This means the characteristic sound of the recording venue, and it is used when describing how well the system and listening environment portray the original venue. Some head units and signal processors have facilities to synthesise the ambient characteristics of different venues.

Ampere
Unit of measurement of electrical current. Used, for instance, to describe alternator output or amplifier current consumption.

Amplifier
See Power Amplifier.

Amplitude
The strength of a signal or a sound, without reference to its frequency content.

Analogue
An audio signal that is an electrical replica of the waveform of the sound it represents. Most car stereo components are analogue in nature, but CD or MD head units use digital signals instead.

Arrival Time
The time it takes a sound to reach the listener from the speaker or speakers. Important in time alignment and good system design.

Attack
Describes the initial impact of a sound produced by an audio system.

Attenuate
To decrease the amplitude – or loudness – of a signal.

Attenuator
A circuit, such as an L-pad, which reduces the level of a signal.

Aux Input
An auxiliary input is generally used to feed a secondary source into a head unit equipped with the required socket.

Backstrap
A metal strip that anchors the rear of an in-dash electronic component to stop it vibrating and to relieve strain on the nose piece.

Baffle
Any panel that is used to mount a speaker becomes the baffle board.

Balance
Generally means the control used to adjust the relative volume between left and right channels of a stereo output.

Balanced Line
A method of audio signal transmission using a cable that doesn't use the outer screen braiding to handle the return portion of the audio signal. Very widely used in professional audio, it isn't common in car stereo systems.

Band
Meaning a specific segment of the audio spectrum. Used when discussing equalisers and crossovers.

Band-Pass Enclosure
A more involved speaker cabinet that uses two chambers to limit the band that passes from the speaker into the listening area. Can be used to eliminate the need for other crossover devices.

Band-Pass Filter
A crossover network that combines low-pass and high-pass components to allow a certain frequency band to pass through.

Bandwidth
A range of frequencies between two limits, which may be applied on purpose – by a crossover – or by technological constraints, as in amplifier bandwidth.

Basket
The support structure that holds a speaker cone and the magnet assembly together in correct alignment.

Bass
Low frequencies, generally up to 100Hz.

Bass-Reflex Enclosure
See Ported Enclosure.

Boomy
Term used to describe inaccurate bass that is overblown or flabby. The opposite of Tight.

Box
An enclosure used to house speakers, generally bass speakers.

Bridge
Bridging is a technique where an amplifier's stereo channels are coupled to produce a single, more powerful mono channel.

Bright
Refers to treble output, generally meaning there is a lot of – possibly too much – treble.

Bus
A wiring method using one multi-core cable to link components together and to the controller, rather than individually back to the controller.

Cabin Gain
The natural boost of the lower frequencies caused by the acoustic properties of the vehicle's interior. Also known as the transfer function.

Capacitor
A device that filters out low frequencies from an audio signal, used in active and passive high-pass filters.

Centre Channel
A third channel used to enhance and reinforce the stereo image in the front of a car. The signal can be derived from joining into both left and right signal, or it can be synthesised in an electronic processor.

Centre Frequency
In an equaliser, the centre frequency is the one affected when a corresponding level control is adjusted. In regular equalisers the centre frequency is fixed, but in parametric equalisers the frequency can be adjusted.

Channel
A discreet path for an audio signal. Stereo systems have two channels – left and right – but a surround-sound system like Dolby 5.1 has six channels.

Channel Separation
A measurement of the amount of leakage between an electronic component's left and right channels. Expressed as a dB figure, and higher figures are better.

Circuit Breaker
A resettable protection device that breaks the current flow when excess amperage is detected. All breakers have an ampere rating, and some automatically reset. (See Fuse.)

Clean
A subjective term meaning distortion-free.

Clipping
A term describing the distortion that occurs when an electronic device cannot accommodate the maximum levels of the input signal.

Coaxial
A speaker design in which two drivers share the same axis. Normally describes a speaker with a woofer and a tweeter suspended in front of it.

Colouration
Some form of unnatural characteristic in the reproduced sound, caused by subtle distortion that results in a change in the timbre of the sound,

without the sound being noticeably distorted.

Conductor
A low-resistance material used for the transfer of electrical current.

Cone
The part of a speaker that produces sound by rapid fore-and-aft movement, so called because of its cone shape. (See Diaphragm.)

Crossover Frequency
In a crossover network, this is the frequency where the signal is divided. Also known as a crossover point or cut-off point.

Crossover Network
An electronic component designed to separate frequency bands from an audio signal and route the appropriate frequencies to the correct drivers.

Current
The flow of electrons through a conductor. In direct current (DC) the electrons flow in one direction, in alternating current (AC) the electrons move in both directions. It is delivered by the battery/alternator system and powers the electrical devices in the vehicle.

Current Draw
The amount of current needed by an electronic component to carry out its function.

D/A converter
The electrical circuit that converts the binary code in a digital signal to its analogue equivalent.

Damping
Refers to how tightly an amplifier or speaker's suspension controls the cone motion. (See Damping Factor.)

Damping Factor
A measurement of an amplifier's ability to control the speaker cone's motion once the signal has died away. Figures above 200 are considered very good.

DAT (Digital Audio Tape)
A cassette that uses magnetic tape to store digital information, now almost totally defunct in the car stereo world. (See DCC.)

dB (deciBel)
The unit used to measure the difference between two levels of sound or electrical signal. This is a logarithmic scale where an increase of 10dB represents a tenfold increase in power. Doubling power raises SPL by approx 3dB, halving power reduces SPL by approx 3dB. (See SPL).

DC (Direct Current)
The current delivered by the vehicle's charging system after rectification.

Digital Compact Cassette (DCC)
Another format where digital signals are recorded on to magnetic tape.

Decay
Describes the audio system's response to a signal when that signal ends.

Depth
Term used to describe the audio system's ability to create a realistic three-dimensional sound stage.

Detachable Face
A security feature of most head units where the control panel can be removed from the body of the unit, making it unattractive to a thief who needs the panel to make the unit work.

Detent
Generally the centre position of a knob or slider, marked on a scale and also felt as a slight resistance to movement either way from that point.

Diaphragm
The part of a speaker that produces sound by vibrating in response to an electrical signal from an amplifier. Can be one of several shapes – cone, dome, flat and planar.

Digital
A component or process that uses a binary code or digits in some form. Can mean a radio that displays its station settings with digits on a screen, but more commonly used in electronic tuning or playback devices.

Digital Output
A jack that offers a digital signal for use in other components in the system.

DIN
The acronym for Deutsche Industrie Normen, and the standard usually used when referring to head unit dimensions as well as some speaker sizes.

DIN Cable
A multi-cored cable that is terminated with a single multi-pin plug at each end. Generally not interchangeable between equipment brands.

Directionality
The change in a speaker's dispersion pattern as the audio frequency rises.

Dispersion
Refers to the output pattern of a speaker. The narrower the pattern, the more directional a speaker is.

Distortion
Any unwanted alteration in an audio signal. Possibly irritating and potentially damaging.

Diversity Tuning
A radio tuning system that uses two antennas and constantly compares the signals from them while playing the best at any time.

DNR (Dynamic Noise Reduction)
A method of reducing background noise in a signal when the playback level is low.

Dolby
Dolby is a registered trademark of the Dolby Laboratories, which designs and produces noise reduction systems and surround-sound processors and electronics.

Dome
A speaker component that produces sound but is dome-shaped rather than cone-shaped. Domes can be made of many different materials and are usually classified by 'soft' or 'hard' depending on what they are made from.

Driver
An individual speaker.

DSP (Digital Signal Process/ing)
A term referring to any signal processor that manipulates the signal in the digital domain. DSP functions can include time alignment, ambience synthesis and filtering.

Dynamic Range
The difference between the maximum signal level attainable and the noise floor of an audio component, expressed in dB.

Earth
See Ground.

Enclosure
Another name for a speaker box. Also known as a cabinet.

Equalisation
The boosting or cutting of audio frequencies by electronic means. Can be done to correct acoustic anomalies or tailor the acoustic signal to the listener's preference.

Equaliser
An electronic component – or section of a component – that divides the audio signal for equalisation purposes. (See also Graphic Equaliser and Parametric Equaliser.)

Fader
A control – either on a head unit or separate from it – used to change the relative volume between front and rear speakers.

Ferrofluid
A ferromagnetic liquid used in some speakers, especially tweeters, to conduct heat away from the voice coil and improve damping and power handling.

Fibre-Optic Link
The cable used to transmit an optical digital signal from one digital component to another.

Fibre Optics
A method of transmitting digital audio signals as pulses of light, through a special cable. The main benefit is immunity from electrical interference.

Fill
Term used to describe ambient information in an audio system. Can originate from front, rear or sides.

Filter
A circuit that boosts, attenuates or removes selected frequencies from an audio signal.

Flat
A 0dB setting – neither boosted nor attenuated – as in equalisers, tone controls and frequency response.

Forced-Air Cooling
A feature found on some amplifiers that uses one or more fans to circulate air through the amplifier and keep the amplifier within its safe thermal limits.

Free-Air
See Infinite Baffle.

Frequency
Described as the rate of vibration or oscillation of sound, it is measured in cycles per second, or Hertz (Hz). The audio spectrum is considered to be 20Hz to 20,000Hz (20kHz).

Frequency Response
Describes how evenly a component or system reproduces frequencies in the audio spectrum. It should be referenced to a dB tolerance figure, and closer tolerances are better.

Front stage
Characteristic in which all music seems to originate from a plane in front of the listening position with no discernible fill from centre or rear speakers.

Full-Range Speaker
A single driver unit that's designed to reproduce all or most of the frequencies between 20 and 20,000Hz.

Fuse
An electrical protection device that prevents damage from occurring by stopping the flow of current through a circuit when the amperage of the current flow is too high. Fuses are available in many ratings but, unlike circuit breakers, they cannot be reset.

Gain
The degree of amplification achieved by an electrical circuit, generally expressed in dB.

Graphic Equaliser
An audio component that breaks down the frequency spectrum into bands, and allows the output of each band to be cut or boosted. Can be very useful to correct frequency anomalies in a system or to tailor a sound to someone's preference.

Grommet
Usually a rubber or plastic bushing that is used to protect a cable as it passes through a surface that could possibly wear away the cable's insulation layer.

Ground
The theoretical zero-voltage reference. Often used to describe a negative power connection to the vehicle's structure, and also the negative terminal on an audio component or the vehicle battery.

Ground Loop
A common condition where an electronic component or system has more than one path to ground. This difference in ground potential will often introduce noise into the system.

Hard Dome
A tweeter dome that is made of a stiff material, such as aluminium or titanium, as opposed to a soft dome made from silk or something similar.

Headroom
The difference, usually expressed in dB, between the highest level present in a signal and the maximum level an audio device can handle without noticeable distortion.

Head Unit
The generic term for a system's source component, such as a CD tuner or radio/cassette player.

Hertz (Hz)
A unit of frequency measurement representing one complete cycle per second. In sound terms, the higher the Hz figure, the higher the sound's pitch.

High Frequency
In audio terms, the frequency range from approximately 5kHz (5000Hz) to 20kHz (20,000Hz).

High-Pass Filter
A crossover circuit that lets through frequencies above the chosen crossover point.

Horn Speaker
A speaker type that uses a flared tube to disperse the sound produced by the driver fitted to the throat of the horn. Most widely seen in Sound Off competition vehicles.

IASCA (International Auto Sound Challenge Association)
An organisation that sanctions Sound Off competitions. Both Sound Quality and Sound Pressure Level contests are offered. The UK affiliated body is the SCA.

Imaging
A system's ability to place vocals and instrumentation in a spatially realistic manner.

Impedance
A measurement, expressed in ohms, of the electrical resistance in a component. The lower the number, the lower the impedance.

Inductor
A coil of wire used to attenuate

high frequencies. A key component in a passive low-pass crossover.

Infinite Baffle
In car audio, a type of speaker installation that uses a sealed compartment of the vehicle, often the boot, to isolate the rear wave of a speaker's output rather than fitting an actual enclosure. Widely used for sub woofers fitted to rear parcel shelves.

Input Sensitivity
Specification that gives the input signal level required for an amplifier to produce its rated output. Input sensitivity is adjustable on many power amplifiers and signal processors.

Installation
The process and methods used to integrate audio system components into a vehicle.

Isobaric
A method of installing woofers using a compound loading technique where a pair of woofers share the same airspace between them. The woofers are either face-to-face or piggybacked. The main benefit is a reduction of airspace needed to mount them.

kHz (kiloHertz)
A thousand Hertz.

Kickpanel
The side of the footwell area, now widely used for custom speaker enclosures.

L-Pad
An arrangement of two resistors designed to attenuate the output level of a driver.

LCD (Liquid Crystal Display)
A type of electronic readout used in head units and some system components.

LED (Light Emitting Diode)
A small light often used as a condition or function indicator on an electronic component.

Linearity
Describes the accuracy of a component's output signal compared to its input signal. Also used to describe how a signal alters as amplitude is increased.

Line Level
The low-voltage audio signal, usually between 500 millivolts and 4 volts, also known as the pre-amp level. This voltage is increased when the signal passes through an amplifier.

Listening Fatigue
Auditory exhaustion caused by listening to high sound levels, high distortion, uneven frequency response, or a combination of the three.

Loudness Control
A control designed to boost the low and high frequencies at low listening levels to compensate for the way the human ear works with quieter sounds.

Low-Pass Filter
A crossover circuit that lets through those frequencies which are below the chosen crossover point.

Magazine
The removable module of a CD autochanger that is loaded with CDs. Can take six, eight, ten or 12 discs, depending on make of 'changer.

Maximum Power
The maximum or peak amount of power an amplifier can produce for a short burst. Maximum ratings are usually accompanied with large amounts of distortion and should generally be ignored.

Mid Bass
The section of the audio spectrum between sub bass and mid range, about 100-400Hz.

Mid Range
The section of the audio spectrum between the mid-bass and the treble, about 400-5000Hz. This important area contains most of the

fundamental tones of the human voice and many musical instruments.

Millivolt (mV)
One thousandth of a volt. A term used when describing low-level signals and component sensitivity.

Mono
An audio signal which has only one channel. No discernible stereo information.

Muddy
A term used to describe a sound, usually in the bass region, that is unclear.

Nasal
A term used to describe a sound, usually in the mid range, which is pinched and unnatural. Often used for poorly reproduced vocals.

Noise
Any unwanted signal component not present in the original input signal but present in the output signal.

Noise Floor
In a component, the noise floor is the residual noise it produces. In a vehicle, it is the background noise produced by the wind, tyres, engine and other vehicles.

Noise Gate
A noise-reduction device inserted in the signal path before the amplification. A noise gate is designed to mute output at a low signal level to eliminate system noise, but incorrect setting can interrupt musical content as well.

Noise Reduction Circuit
A method of reducing noise inherent in analogue tape recordings. Best known systems are Dolby B, Dolby C, DNR, and dbx.

Octave
The interval between two frequencies, where the higher frequency is twice that of the lower one. The audible frequency bandwidth covers 20Hz to 20kHz, which is broken up into ten octaves.

OEM (Original Equipment Manufacturer)
Also known as stock, OEM describes any factory-installed equipment offered in a vehicle.

Off-Axis
A listening or test-microphone position that is not directly in front of a speaker.

Ohm
A unit of electrical resistance or impedance.

On-Axis
A listening or test-microphone position that is directly in front of a speaker.

Oversampling Rate
A digital filtering technique used in all CD components. Extra data points are mathematically interpolated between those read from the disc, creating a signal at a multiple of the original 44.1kHz sampling frequency (usually two, four or eight times).

Parallel Wiring
A wiring scheme that decreases the impedance of the speaker load seen by an amplifier, thus increasing the power delivered to the speakers.

Parametric Equaliser
An equalisation component that has an adjustable centre frequency, allowing very fine tailoring of a specific frequency band. May also have adjustable width (Q) to make the chosen band very narrow or very wide.

Pass-Band
The frequency segment allowed through a band-pass filter.

Passive Crossover
A network of capacitors and/or inductors (also known as caps and coils) that divide an audio signal after amplification.

Phase
Describes the relative position of one waveform to another.

Phase-Reversal Switch
A control used to reverse the polarity of a speaker or pair of speakers. Often used on sub woofer(s), the aim is to reinforce output.

Phono Connector
See RCA Connector.

Pink Noise
A random mixture of all audio frequencies having equal energy in each octave. Used as a signal source when measuring frequency response with an electronic device such as a real time analyser, or RTA.

Polarity
The property or characteristic of having two opposing poles. In an electrical system they are known as positive and negative.

Port
The tuned opening in a ported or vented speaker cabinet.

Ported Enclosure
An enclosure design in which the sound waves produced by the rear of the woofer cone are allowed to pass through a port, or vent, in the enclosure to reinforce bass output.

Power Amplifier
Any device which can increase the voltage or current of an electrical signal *and* is the final gain stage of an audio system which directly drives a speaker or speakers with AC voltage.

Preamplifier
A component or part of a component that processes line-level audio signals. All head units have a preamplifier section that usually provides volume, tone, balance and fader controls.

Presence
A subjective term used to describe clarity and realism, usually in the mid range.

Processor (Signal)
A component used to alter an electronic signal in an audio system. Preamps, active crossovers, equalisers, time alignment units, bass restoration devices and surround sound units are all examples of these.

Q
In an equaliser, Q specifies the width of the frequency band relative to its level. The higher the number, the narrower the band or affected frequencies.

Quasi-Parametric Equaliser
An equaliser that allows the user to adjust the centre frequency of the equalised bands, but not their Q.

RCA Connector
The most common form of signal plug used in car audio. It uses a coaxial cable and has a single central pin for the positive signal with a grounded sleeve to complete the circuit.

Rear Stage
Characteristic in which all the music seems to originate from behind the listening position, with no discernible content from the front speakers. Not a realistic or desirable set-up.

Relay
An electromagnetic switch.

Remote Turn-On Lead
A wire coming from the back of most head units that activates another component whenever the head unit is switched on.

Resistor
A raw electronic component that 'resists' current.

Resonance
The vibration, buzzing or ringing of an object or circuit at a particular frequency.

Reverberation
Numerous reflections of sound that arrive at the listener close together and cannot be perceived as individual echoes.

Can be beneficial in creating the illusion of ambience and spaciousness. Can also detract from the impact of bass response if excessive.

Reverse Polarity
An electrical condition in which the positive and negative wires running to one speaker in a stereo pair are reversed. This can cause weaker bass performance, but can also be beneficial in improving a system's staging characteristics.

RMS (Root Mean Square)
A mathematical process for calculating AC current or voltage. Sometimes incorrectly used to refer to the continuous average power output of an amplifier (RMS power).

Roll-Off
A gradual reduction in signal level, above or below a certain frequency, either natural due to design limitations, or intentional through use of a filter. Usually specified in dB per octave.

RTA (Real Time Analyser)
An electronic measuring device for identifying the individual audio frequency bands in a system or environment and displaying their relative levels simultaneously.

Sampling Rate
The number of times per second, expressed in kiloHertz, that a digital signal is divided and then represented as a number indicating its instantaneous amplitude. The basic sampling rate of a CD is 44.1kHz.

Satellites
The speakers – usually a mid woofer and a tweeter, and usually installed in the front of the vehicle –– that are paired with one or more sub woofers in a multi-speaker system.

Sealed Box
See Acoustic-Suspension Enclosure.

Sensitivity
A speaker measurement that tells how much sound (in dB) is produced at a specified distance from the speaker (usually one metre) when it is fed with a specified input signal (usually 2.83 volts, or one watt). Higher numbers are better.

Separation
See Channel Separation.

Series Wiring
A speaker wiring scheme that increases load impedance, decreasing power delivered to the speakers.

Signal
The organised electronic impulses that carry musical information for processing in an audio system.

Signal-To-Noise Ratio
The specification that indicates how much audio signal there is relative to the noise, under specified conditions. It is the ratio of total audio output level to the noise level, expressed in dB.

Signal Processor
A component that in some way manipulates audio signals.

Slope
The rate at which a crossover attenuates out-of-band frequencies, expressed in dB per octave. Typical slopes are six, 12, 18 and 24dB per octave, with 12dB probably being the most common. The higher the number, the steeper the slope, the faster the attenuation occurs.

Sound Linearity
Overall balance of all frequencies with no attenuated frequency or group of frequencies.

Sound Stage
The illusion of a three-dimensional sound field created by a correctly installed and adjusted audio system, in which the individual instruments are in their proper locations, and there

is a proper amount of ambient effect to create depth and width.

Source
An electronic component capable of creating or reproducing a signal.

Speaker
An electromechanical device that converts electrical energy into acoustical energy (sound waves).

Spider
A ring that supports the inner edge of a speaker's cone.

SPL (Sound Pressure Level)
A measurement of acoustic energy, expressed in dB.

Staging
The perceived point of origin of a musical signal in relation to the listener.

Stereo
The use of at least two channels – left and right.

Stereo Image
Accurate reproduction of a musical performance, in which placement of individual instruments are retained by nature of speaker placement, varying proportions of left and right channels, and phase response. Good imaging gives the illusion of no identifiable speaker location.

Subsonic
Frequencies below the lower limit of audibility, which is 20Hz.

Subsonic Filter
A type of high-pass filter used in some signal processors to attenuate frequencies below about 20Hz.

Sub Woofer
A loudspeaker designed to reproduce the lowest frequencies produced by an audio system. Typically less than 100Hz.

Surround
A rubber or foam ring that fills the space between a speaker's

basket and cone, supporting the outer edge of the cone.

Surround Sound
Used to describe the simulation of ambience. 'Surround' systems must have at least four channels (two front, two rear) and now many have six (two front, one centre, two rear and one sub).

Template
A pattern used as a guide for positioning or cutting during an audio system installation.

Thermal Overload
A condition in which a large amount of heat is generated inside an amplifier. Many amps employ protection circuitry that suspends their operation when this occurs.

Thin
Used to describe a range of frequencies that are incorrectly reproduced, usually characterised by a lack of upper bass and/or lower mid range.

Tight
A subjective term used to describe bass reproduction that is well defined or damped.

Transients
An instantaneous peak, or very short-duration signal, present in the signal and reproduced by an audio system.

Transparent
A subjective term used to describe a component that passes audio signals without adding colourations or noise.

Treble
The upper segment of the audio frequency spectrum.

Turn-On Thump
An audible thump that may occur when a component is powered up. Thumps are caused by a brief surge in the component's power supply.

Tweaking
The process of fine-tuning a system for optimum performance.

Tweeter
A type of speaker designed to reproduce high frequencies, from 4kHz upwards.

Ultrasonic
Frequencies above the upper limit of audibility, which is 20kHz.

Valet Switch
In car audio, a security device that prevents the system from being used. In car security, a switch that temporarily prevents the security system from arming.

Vent
See Port.

Vented Enclosure
See Ported Enclosure.

Voice Coil
The coil of wire in the speaker's magnetic field through which amplified signals pass. This causes the speaker's cone or dome to move and make sound.

Volt
Measurement unit of voltage.

Watt
Measurement unit of electrical power. One watt equals one joule of energy per second.

Wire Loom
Used to describe a variety of products that organise and bundle wires for a cleaner appearance and safer installation.

Woofer
A low-frequency driver, usually designed to produce sound frequencies between 100Hz and 500Hz.

Xmax
In a speaker, the peak linear excursion of the voice coil, usually expressed in millimetres.

Index

Haynes Car Manuals

Haynes Manuals

Alfa Romeo Alfasud/Sprint (74 - 88)	0292
Alfa Romeo Alfetta (73 - 87)	0531
Audi 80 (72 - Feb 79)	0207
Audi 80, 90 (79 - Oct 86) & Coupe (81 - Nov 88)	0605
Audi 80, 90 (Oct 86 - 90) & Coupe (Nov 88 - 90)	1491
Audi 100 (Oct 82 - 90) & 200 (Feb 84 - Oct 89)	0907
Audi 100 & A6 Petrol & Diesel (May 91 - May 97)	3504
Audi A4 (95 - Feb 00)	3575
Austin A35 & A40 (56 - 67)	0118
Austin Allegro 1100, 1300, 1.0, 1.1 & 1.3 (73 - 82)	0164
Austin Healey 100/6 & 3000 (56 - 68)	0049
Austin/MG/Rover Maestro 1.3 & 1.6 (83 - 95)	0922
Austin/MG Metro (80 - May 90)	0718
Austin/Rover Montego 1.3 & 1.6 (84 - 94)	1066
Austin/MG/Rover Montego 2.0 (84 - 95)	1067
Austin/Rover 2.0 litre Diesel Engine (86 - 93)	1857
Bedford CF (69 - 87)	0163
Bedford/Vauxhall Rascal & Suzuki Supercarry (86 - Oct 94)	3015
BMW 1500, 1502, 1600, 1602, 2000 & 2002 (59 - 77)	0240
BMW 316, 320 & 320i (4-cyl) (75 - Feb 83)	0276
BMW 320, 320i, 323i & 325i (6-cyl) (Oct 77 - Sept 87)	0815
BMW 3-Series (Apr 91 - 96)	3210
BMW 3- & 5-Series (sohc)(81 - 91)	1948
BMW 520i & 525e (Oct 81 - June 88)	1560
BMW 525, 528 & 528i (73 - Sept 81)	0632
Citroën 2CV, Ami & Dyane (67 - 90)	0196
Citroën AX Petrol & Diesel (87 - 97)	3014
Citroën BX (83 - 94)	0908
Citroën C15 Van Petrol & Diesel (89 - Oct 98)	3509
Citroën CX (75 - 88)	0528
Citroën Saxo Petrol & Diesel (96 - 01)	3506
Citroën Visa (79 - 88)	0620
Citroën Xantia Petrol & Diesel (93 - 98)	3082
Citroën XM Petrol & Diesel (89 - 98)	3451
Citroën Xsara Petrol & Diesel (97 - Sept 00)	3751
Citroën ZX Diesel (91 - 98)	1922
Citroën ZX Petrol (91 - 98)	1881
Citroën 1.7 & 1.9 litre Diesel Engine (84 - 96)	1379
Fiat 126 (73 - 87)	0305
Fiat 500 (57 - 73)	0090
Fiat Bravo & Brava (95 - 00)	3572
Fiat Cinquecento (93 - 98)	3501
Fiat Panda (81 - 95)	0793
Fiat Punto Petrol & Diesel (94 - Oct 99)	3251
Fiat Regata (84 - 88)	1167
Fiat Tipo (88 - 91)	1625
Fiat Uno (83 - 95)	0923
Fiat X1/9 (74 - 89)	0273
Ford Anglia (59 - 68)	0001
Ford Capri II (& III) 1.6 & 2.0 (74 - 87)	0283
Ford Capri II (& III) 2.8 & 3.0 (74 - 87)	1309
Ford Cortina Mk III 1300 & 1600 (70 - 76)	0070
Ford Cortina Mk IV (& V) 1.6 & 2.0 (76 - 83)	0343
Ford Cortina Mk IV (& V) 2.3 V6 (77 - 83)	0426
Ford Escort Mk I 1100 & 1300 (68 - 74)	0171
Ford Escort Mk I Mexico, RS 1600 & RS 2000 (70 - 74)	0139
Ford Escort Mk II Mexico, RS 1800 & RS 2000 (75 - 80)	0735
Ford Escort (75 - Aug 80)	0280
Ford Escort (Sept 80 - Sept 90)	0686
Ford Escort & Orion (Sept 90 - 00)	1737
Ford Fiesta (76 - Aug 83)	0334
Ford Fiesta (Aug 83 - Feb 89)	1030
Ford Fiesta (Feb 89 - Oct 95)	1595
Ford Fiesta (Oct 95 - 01)	3397
Ford Focus (98 - 01)	3759
Ford Granada (Sept 77 - Feb 85)	0481
Ford Granada & Scorpio (Mar 85 - 94)	1245
Ford Ka (96 - 99)	3570
Ford Mondeo Petrol (93 - 99)	1923
Ford Mondeo Diesel (93 - 96)	3465
Ford Orion (83 - Sept 90)	1009
Ford Sierra 4 cyl. (82 - 93)	0903
Ford Sierra V6 (82 - 91)	0904
Ford Transit Petrol (Mk 2) (78 - Jan 86)	0719
Ford Transit Petrol (Mk 3) (Feb 86 - 89)	1468
Ford Transit Diesel (Feb 86 - 99)	3019
Ford 1.6 & 1.8 litre Diesel Engine (84 - 96)	1172
Ford 2.1, 2.3 & 2.5 litre Diesel Engine (77 - 90)	1606
Freight Rover Sherpa (74 - 87)	0463
Hillman Avenger (70 - 82)	0037
Hillman Imp (63 - 76)	0022
Honda Accord (76 - Feb 84)	0351
Honda Civic (Feb 84 - Oct 87)	1226
Honda Civic (Nov 91 - 96)	3199
Hyundai Pony (85 - 94)	3398
Jaguar E Type (61 - 72)	0140
Jaguar Mkl & II, 240 & 340 (55 - 69)	0098

Jaguar XJ6, XJ & Sovereign; Daimler Sovereign (68 - Oct 86)	0242
Jaguar XJ6 & Sovereign (Oct 86 - Sept 94)	3261
Jaguar XJ12, XJS & Sovereign; Daimler Double Six (72 - 88)	0478
Jeep Cherokee Petrol (93 - 96)	1943
Lada 1200, 1300, 1500 & 1600 (74 - 91)	0413
Lada Samara (87 - 91)	1610
Land Rover 90, 110 & Defender Diesel (83 - 95)	3017
Land Rover Discovery Petrol & Diesel (89 - 98)	3016
Land Rover Series IIA & III Diesel (58 - 85)	0529
Land Rover Series II, IIA & III Petrol (58 - 85)	0314
Mazda 323 (Mar 81 - Oct 89)	1608
Mazda 323 (Oct 89 - 98)	3455
Mazda 626 (May 83 - Sept 87)	0929
Mazda B-1600, B-1800 & B-2000 Pick-up (72 - 88)	0267
Mazda RX-7 (79 - 85)	0460
Mercedes-Benz 190, 190E & 190D Petrol & Diesel (83 - 93)	3450
Mercedes-Benz 200, 240, 300 Diesel (Oct 76 - 85)	1114
Mercedes-Benz 250 & 280 (68 - 72)	0346
Mercedes-Benz 250 & 280 (123 Series) (Oct 76 - 84)	0677
Mercedes-Benz 124 Series (85 - Aug 93)	3253
Mercedes-Benz C-Class Petrol & Diesel (93 - Aug 00)	3511
MGA (55 - 62)	0475
MGB (62 - 80)	0111
MG Midget & AH Sprite (58 - 80)	0265
Mini (59 - 69)	0527
Mini (69 - Oct 96)	0646
Mitsubishi Shogun & L200 Pick-Ups (83 - 94)	1944
Morris Ital 1.3 (80 - 84)	0705
Morris Minor 1000 (56 - 71)	0024
Nissan Bluebird (May 84 - Mar 86)	1223
Nissan Bluebird (Mar 86 - 90)	1473
Nissan Cherry (Sept 82 - 86)	1031
Nissan Micra (83 - Jan 93)	0931
Nissan Micra (93 - 99)	3254
Nissan Primera (90 - Aug 99)	1851
Nissan Stanza (82 - 86)	0824
Nissan Sunny (May 82 - Oct 86)	0895
Nissan Sunny (Oct 86 - Mar 91)	1378
Nissan Sunny (Apr 91 - 95)	3219
Opel Ascona & Manta (B Series) (Sept 75 - 88)	0316
Opel Kadett (Nov 79 - Oct 84)	0634
Opel Rekord (Feb 78 - Oct 86)	0543
Peugeot 106 Petrol & Diesel (91 - 01)	1882
Peugeot 205 Petrol (83 - 97)	0932
Peugeot 206 Petrol and Diesel (98 - 01)	3757
Peugeot 305 (78 - 89)	0538
Peugeot 306 Petrol & Diesel (93 - 99)	3073
Peugeot 309 (86 - 93)	1266
Peugeot 405 Petrol (88 - 97)	1559
Peugeot 405 Diesel (88 - 97)	3198
Peugeot 406 Petrol & Diesel (96 - 97)	3394
Peugeot 505 (79 - 89)	0762
Peugeot 1.7/1.8 & 1.9 litre Diesel Engine (82 - 96)	0950
Peugeot 2.0, 2.1, 2.3 & 2.5 litre Diesel Engines (74 - 90)	1607
Porsche 911 (65 - 85)	0264
Porsche 924 & 924 Turbo (76 - 85)	0397
Proton (89 - 97)	3255
Range Rover V8 (70 - Oct 92)	0606
Reliant Robin & Kitten (73 - 83)	0436
Renault 4 (61 - 86)	0072
Renault 5 (Feb 85 - 96)	1219
Renault 9 & 11 (82 - 89)	0822
Renault 18 (79 - 86)	0598
Renault 19 Petrol (89 - 94)	1646
Renault 19 Diesel (89 - 95)	1946
Renault 21 (86 - 94)	1397
Renault 25 (84 - 92)	1228
Renault Clio Petrol (91 - May 98)	1853
Renault Clio Diesel (91 - June 96)	3031
Renault Clio Petrol & Diesel (May 98 - May 01)	3906
Renault Espace Petrol & Diesel (85 - 96)	3197
Renault Fuego (80 - 86)	0764
Renault Laguna Petrol & Diesel (94 - 00)	3252
Renault Mégane & Scénic Petrol & Diesel (96 - 98)	3395
Rover 213 & 216 (84 - 89)	1116
Rover 214 & 414 (89 - 96)	1689
Rover 216 & 416 (89 - 96)	1830
Rover 211, 214, 216, 218 & 220 Petrol & Diesel (Dec 95 - 98)	3399
Rover 414, 416 & 420 Petrol & Diesel (May 95 - 98)	3453
Rover 618, 620 & 623 (93 - 97)	3257
Rover 820, 825 & 827 (86 - 95)	1380
Rover 3500 (76 - 87)	0365
Rover Metro, 111 & 114 (May 90 - 98)	1711
Saab 90, 99 & 900 (79 - Oct 93)	0765
Saab 95 & 96 (66 - 76)	0198
Saab 99 (69 - 79)	0247

Saab 900 (Oct 93 - 98)	3512
Saab 9000 (4-cyl) (85 - 98)	1686
Seat Ibiza & Cordoba Petrol & Diesel (Oct 93 - Oct 99)	3571
Seat Ibiza & Malaga (85 - 92)	1609
Skoda Estelle (77 - 89)	0604
Skoda Favorit (89 - 96)	1801
Skoda Felicia Petrol & Diesel (95 - 99)	3505
Subaru 1600 & 1800 (Nov 79 - 90)	0995
Sunbeam Alpine, Rapier & H120 (67 - 76)	0051
Suzuki Supercarry (86 - Oct 94)	3015
Suzuki SJ Series, Samurai & Vitara (4-cyl) (82 - 97)	1942
Talbot Alpine, Solara, Minx & Rapier (75 - 86)	0337
Talbot Horizon (78 - 86)	0473
Talbot Samba (82 - 86)	0823
Toyota Carina E (May 92 - 97)	3256
Toyota Corolla (Sept 83 - Sept 87)	1024
Toyota Corolla (80 - 85)	0683
Toyota Corolla (Sept 87 - Aug 92)	1683
Toyota Corolla (Aug 92 - 97)	3259
Toyota Hi-Ace & Hi-Lux (69 - Oct 83)	0304
Triumph Acclaim (81 - 84)	0792
Triumph GT6 & Vitesse (62 - 74)	0112
Triumph Herald (59 - 71)	0010
Triumph Spitfire (62 - 81)	0113
Triumph Stag (70 - 78)	0441
Triumph TR2, 3, 3A, 4 & 4A (52 - 67)	0028
Triumph TR5 & 6 (67 - 75)	0031
Triumph TR7 (75 - 82)	0322
Vauxhall Astra (80 - Oct 84)	0635
Vauxhall Astra & Belmont (Oct 84 - Oct 91)	1136
Vauxhall Astra (Oct 91 - Feb 98)	1832
Vauxhall/Opel Astra & Zafira Diesel (Feb 98 - Sept 00)	3797
Vauxhall/Opel Astra & Zafira Petrol (Feb 98 - Sept 00)	3758
Vauxhall/Opel Calibra (90 - 98)	3502
Vauxhall Carlton (Oct 78 - Oct 86)	0480
Vauxhall Carlton & Senator (Nov 86 - 94)	1469
Vauxhall Cavalier 1300 (77 - July 81)	0461
Vauxhall Cavalier 1600, 1900 & 2000 (75 - July 81)	0315
Vauxhall Cavalier (81 - Oct 88)	0812
Vauxhall Cavalier (Oct 88 - 95)	1570
Vauxhall Chevette (75 - 84)	0285
Vauxhall Corsa (Mar 93 - 97)	1985
Vauxhall/Opel Frontera Petrol & Diesel (91 - Sept 98)	3454
Vauxhall Nova (83 - 93)	0909
Vauxhall/Opel Omega (94 - 99)	3510
Vauxhall Vectra Petrol & Diesel (95 - 98)	3396
Vauxhall/Opel 1.5, 1.6 & 1.7 litre Diesel Engine (82 - 96)	1222
Volkswagen 411 & 412 (68 - 75)	0091
Volkswagen Beetle 1200 (54 - 77)	0036
Volkswagen Beetle 1300 & 1500 (65 - 75)	0039
Volkswagen Beetle 1302 & 1302S (70 - 72)	0110
Volkswagen Beetle 1303, 1303S & GT (72 - 75)	0159
Volkswagen Beetle (Apr 99 - 01)	3798
Volkswagen Golf & Jetta Mk 1 1.1 & 1.3 (74 - 84)	0716
Volkswagen Golf, Jetta & Scirocco Mk 1 1.5, 1.6 & 1.8 (74 - 84)	0726
Volkswagen Golf & Jetta Mk 1 Diesel (78 - 84)	0451
Volkswagen Golf & Jetta Mk 2 (Mar 84 - Feb 92)	1081
Volkswagen Golf & Vento Petrol & Diesel (Feb 92 - 96)	3097
Volkswagen Golf & Bora Petrol & Diesel (April 98 - 00)	3727
Volkswagen LT vans & light trucks (76 - 87)	0637
Volkswagen Passat & Santana (Sept 81 - May 88)	0814
Volkswagen Passat Petrol & Diesel (May 88 - 96)	3498
Volkswagen Polo & Derby (76 - Jan 82)	0335
Volkswagen Polo (82 - Oct 90)	0813
Volkswagen Polo (Nov 90 - Aug 94)	3245
Volkswagen Polo Hatchback Petrol & Diesel (94 - 99)	3500
Volkswagen Scirocco (82 - 90)	1224
Volkswagen Transporter 1600 (68 - 79)	0082
Volkswagen Transporter 1700, 1800 & 2000 (72 - 79)	0226
Volkswagen Transporter (air-cooled) (79 - 82)	0638
Volkswagen Transporter (water-cooled) (82 - 90)	3452
Volkswagen Type 3 (63 - 73)	0084
Volvo 120 & 130 Series (& P1800)(61 - 73)	0203
Volvo 142, 144 & 145 (66 - 74)	0129
Volvo 240 Series (74 - 93)	0270
Volvo 262, 264 & 260/265 (75 - 85)	0400
Volvo 340, 343, 345 & 360 (76 - 91)	0715
Volvo 440, 460 & 480 (87 - 97)	1691
Volvo 740 & 760 (82 - 91)	1258
Volvo 850 (92 - 96)	3260
Volvo 940 (90 - 96)	3249
Volvo S40 & V40 (96 - 99)	3569
Volvo S70, V70 & C70 (96 - 99)	3573

Haynes Car Service and Repair Manuals are available from car accessory retailers.
For further information or to find your nearest stockist, call
01963 442030 or visit
www.haynes.co.uk